86 Days in Greece

86 Days in Greece

A Time of Crisis

Taso Lagos

English Hill Press

Redmond, WA

"The Monastery of Predictions" is a work of fiction. Any resemblance to actual events, places, or persons living or dead, is entirely coincidental.

Published by English Hill Press
P.O. Box 8521
Kirkland, WA 98034

Cover design by Barbara Silbert; cover photography by George Vthokakis; text design by David E. Schultz.

First Edition
1 3 5 7 9 8 6 4 2

ISBN13 978-0-9846543-2-1

This book is dedicated to my grandmother, Evangelia Gerali and to all the people of Greece who have suffered but endure.

86 Days in Greece

Preface

When I returned to the U.S. after spending nearly three months in Greece in spring, 2012, I was asked by friends if the economic crisis was as bad as the media said. Will Greece survive? Can Greece bring down the entire world if it defaults on its crushing debt?

I struggled to answer my friends, but then I remembered the blog I started with my former student Samson X. Lim. The blog was intended to keep a daily account of my study-abroad program in Northern Greece. While there, and as the days stumbled along, I found myself keeping a diary not only of the student group's activities, but of Greece itself. Perhaps I could answer my friends' questions by publishing the blogs that I kept for those 86 days.

I wrote as an eyewitness to the events around me, captured those events and made observations in the form of snapshots that meant to both explain the unfolding situation in Greece and reveal what the country was like at that particularly historic moment.

We live in history all the time, but we are not conscious of it. Only when we read about it does it become "historical." Otherwise, it's just a day—we get up, we brush our teeth, we shower, we work, we eat, we relax, we go to sleep.

But even as I went through the events of my day, it became increasingly obvious that Greece was being transformed. The great events of the day—the national elections, the economic reforms, the growing skepticism on the part of Greece's international lenders that the country could be saved, talk of Greece's exit from the euro currency, etc.—created an atmosphere of profound change.

Each new dawn seemed to bring a major development for Greece; it felt as if the country was either going to collapse or give birth to a new society. Each day these two titanic forces wrestled and fought, with the outcome still uncertain. There seemed no middle ground. The only way I could explain the forces taking place around me was to refer both to my personal experience, having been born in the country, and also as a scholar fascinated by modern Greece.

Modern Greece's history is a complicated entanglement. Briefly, it begins in 1821 when Greeks fought for independence from their Ottoman Empire subjugators. Since 1453, from a dark day in Greek history when the Ottomans sacked Constantinople and took control of a vast swatch of territory from what is now Bulgaria to parts of the Middle East, it had been the dream of Greeks to liberate themselves.

During the Ottoman occupation, the Greek community was ruled by the Greek Orthodox Church according to the "millet" system. Rather than exercising direct control of its territories, the Ottomans appointed members of a specific ethnic community to be its government. For Greeks, it was the Church.

This system worked more or less effectively, and in doing so brought prestige to the Church. Yet it was the same Church that in 1453 replaced their colorful robes with black ones that symbolized the horror of losing Constantinople to the Turks.

When revolutionary fervor was in the air, thanks in part to members of the Greek diaspora in places like London, Paris and Vienna in the late 1700s and early 1800s, the Church was slow to react. It took some years and a few successful battles before the Church got behind the effort.

By 1830, Greece was born. But it was born into a crazy family. Many historians today feel that the birth of modern Greece was a botched operation—not only was there infighting among the groups that led the revolution against the Turks, but the Great Powers that helped them in their fight for freedom (England, France, and Russia) made their own demands.

The first leader of Greece was assassinated, and finally to settle what was becoming a political nightmare, a young prince from Bavaria was brought in to rule. The association between Greece and Germany, which has a long and tangled history, began.

Despite new-found freedom, it was a devastatingly poor and wretched country. Centuries of Ottoman rule and stagnancy left the country a backward agricultural nation ill-suited for the modern era. If Greece is primarily known for its emigrants, and there are millions over the past two centuries, it is because there was simply not enough work, or even food, to feed itself at the time of its birth.

The Greek economy collapsed in the early 1890s, sending hundreds of thousands abroad. Many came to the United States. Those that stayed behind, found life unusually harsh. With the coming of War World I, political chaos in Greece increased. In 1922 it suffered a military setback in Turkey that resulted in the destruction of the Greek community in Smyrna.

World War II brought further calamities. Greece suffered an invasion by Hitler's forces, and in 1945, while the rest of Europe began the long tedious march towards recovery after the devastating war, it plunged into a Civil War that put the country back decades. In a certain sense, it is still recovering from that epic period. The political divide that resulted in the Civil War—between left-wing progressives and conservative traditionalists—has never been resolved. It still plays out in peculiar ways today.

The 1950s saw Greece taking small steps towards recovery. In the mid 1950s, the economies of Greece and South Korea, for example, were comparatively on par. But while Korea's economy soon took off, Greece's remained backward. Even the economic help of the Marshall Plan and American advisors assisting the effort could not bring Greece toward serious development.

Eventually, it was tourism that saved the day. Films about Greece helped to publicize the quiet, simple, and one must say, cheap, lifestyle that brought in hordes of visitors. Even the brutal overthrow of Greek democracy in 1967 by a group of buffoonish colonels did not dampen enthusiasm for travelers to Greece. Democracy was restored in 1974 after a badly planned and disastrous attempt by the dictators to annex Cyprus in a military putsch. This led to the invasion of Cyprus by Turkey and the now permanent division of the island between Greek and Turkish sectors.

In 1981, Greece was admitted into the European Union, and the economic development that had long escaped it, as far back as 1930, finally seemed to become a reality. E.U. funds came pouring in and resulted in new roads and infrastructure projects, as well as greater mobility of Greek exports to the rest of Europe. Tourism boomed. By the 1990s, Greece seemed on the verge of becoming another one of the smart, successful European nations fast ticking into the global economic system.

In 2004, it successfully hosted the Olympic Games in Athens. The effort and money spent to ready the city for the Games was heroic, but it was also devastating to the finances of the country. It added billions to Greece's debt. This may have gone unnoticed, but when the world suddenly fell into a recession in 2008, Greece's horrendous debts could no longer be hidden. A giant game of chicken had been played for decades, with government officials hiding the full extent of the borrowing and corruption; so when the day of reckoning came in 2009, the blow landed hard.

Today, Greece is in the throes of an economic depression. Its unemployment rate sits at 28%, highest in Europe. Many Greeks have lost jobs and businesses, for the economy bled 1000 workers per day during the crisis. Others fled the country, seeking work elsewhere—ironically enough, even in Germany. Many Greeks blame Germany for its economic ills (they blame the country for stealing all its money during War World II and for imposing harsh measures to stay out of bankruptcy in its present predicament).

There have been many riots since 2009, with images beaming around the world of a deeply divided, chaotic country. Tourists have stayed away in droves. The economy slides further with each passing day, and the political class itself is not sure how to move forward. Prime Minister Antonis Samaras wants to stay in the Eurozone and be part of a European solution, while other parties in Greece clamor to get out of the E.U. and chart an independent course.

It is an extraordinary period in the nation's history. In such a period when history seems to speed up and large events happen at a quickened pace, it is dizzying to make sense of it all. Yet this is what I have tried to do with these entries, as a witness to history being made.

Introduction

Many social commentators asked as the Greek crisis unfolded: How is it that a small nation of 10.8 million souls suddenly seems to be the make-or-break element of the entire global economy? Daily news and observation offered us a steady stream of warnings: If Greece goes bankrupt, if Greece leaves the Eurozone, if Greece is kicked out of the European Union, then one of a number of scenarios might happen:

1. The global economy will rupture.
2. The euro currency will collapse.
3. The European Union will disintegrate.

In other words, the world might nearly come to an end.

I had been coming to Greece for many years, leading study-abroad programs, but 2012 and 2013 were the first years I decided to really observe my surroundings and try to make sense of what was happening around me.

The factors that led to Greece facing huge debts and economic meltdown are deep and complex. There is no need to repeat them here; what can be added, however, is that Greece's current economic crisis is not an isolated phenomenon. If it were merely an issue of loans and debt that led to the crisis, the solutions would come from that same arena.

The problems that created the mess have long and ingrained ties in social relations, politics, geography, globalization, and environment. My observations hopefully capture this multi-faceted quality. What must be stressed is that this book does not offer obvious solutions, although at times I offer my thoughts about what can and should be done.

I am not merely an innocent bystander. As someone born in Greece, I return to this country with both a personal as well as an academic interest. My family moved to the United States when I was eight. We lived in a tiny village on the eastern seaboard of the Aegean island of Euboea (also written as Evia). We came to the U.S. as most other immigrants come, because we wanted a better _____ (fill in the blank) future for ourselves, whether economic, social, educational, political, etc.

While I grew up and eventually took my U.S. citizenship, I also stayed very much in contact with the old country. Regular visits to the village were eventually punctuated by becoming a volunteer for the Athens 2004 Olympic Games. I always felt guilty that I did not do my required military training, as all Greek males do, so volunteering was my way of paying back Greece for being a citizen.

It was a transformative moment in my life. From that experience, I decided to set up a study-abroad program to Greece through the University of Washington.

So, beginning in 2005 I started leading groups of students to Greece to learn about the culture, to gain some appreciation of the land and the people, and to think of themselves as global citizens. Not all students came for that purpose, but enough did to make the event a truly fulfilling one for me.

My dissertation dealt with the introduction of new communication technology. I have continued to conduct research in Greece or at home in Greek-related matters. I am also involved in research on the Greek diaspora, particularly in the United States.

While media coverage of the events in Greece tend to focus on the economic and the social (as in the demonstrations and riots), there is another picture that is less seen, which is what I try to reveal here. So I try to go behind the facile images of media and see what's really going on. Does this make me a journalist?

I'm not sure, since these entries are written less with a journalistic purpose in mind and more out of an attempt to make sense of what I was observing. Perhaps that is journalism of a fashion. If so, it's not one that normally appears in newspapers and electronic media.

Perspective is the key, and you are asked to keep this in the back of your mind as you read. Some call this advocacy journalism, and this may be the case here; I am advocating a particular viewpoint of the world, and I need to make this clear from the beginning.

1. Events are not isolated, nor do they take place in a vacuum. A political event, the signing of a bill or a new law, may seem distant and irrelevant, but most human affairs and events are multidimensional and impact different spheres of our lives. In that sense, human events must be regarded in context.

2. Life in one form or another has to be lived. What happens in the stock market may affect our pocketbooks, but we must still attend to our daily tasks and live out our lives as best we can. The question is: how are daily events impacted by large historical events? Whenever there is a riot in Athens, does the social fabric change in any measurable way? Many of the entries here try to explore this question, or at least allude to it.

3. We strive for improvement, whether we acknowledge it or not. This is a basic premise to my thinking behind this book; human beings always try to improve their lives, whether to escape a war zone or get ahead in business. If we didn't want our lives to get better, there would be no problem about Greek pensioners having their monthly stipend reduced, or the wages of the Greek ministers cut by 30% (as Greek Prime Minister Antonis Samaras did shortly after taking office in June 2012).

4. Greek democracy is different from other nations' versions. In America, few protest anymore; the great age of demonstrations (the 1960s) has long passed and the new generation seems

as apolitical as it is possible to become. In Greece, the opposite is true; most people, including the young, are very political—not in the sense of actually being involved in local politics in a positive, productive and regular basis, but political in the sense of endlessly arguing and going out on strikes or marches when asked to do so. This happens in many places in Europe as well (Italy and Spain readily come to mind). This is not a defect, it's a fact. For many, it can be inspiring. You may come to your own conclusion.

5. We must move beyond stereotypes. It is a sad fact of newspaper coverage that stereotypes are used as a kind of short-hand to get a specific point across. If you stop to think about it, in a way it makes sense—articles are not that long and thus there is little space for the journalist to tell the story. Stereotypes are useful for getting to the point. But while useful, they are also corrosive. Which explains the endless stories involving the Greek economic meltdown that mentioned Greeks as lazy and spoiled. A little research on the Internet will reveal that Greeks work more hours than most Europeans (but are less productive) and if they seem spoiled (e.g., taking naps in the afternoons), you try working in 110-degree Fahrenheit.

6. I am predisposed to seeing the goodness and decency in people. This may be a moral outgrowth of my religious back-ground, but it's also something that colors my view of the world. I don't believe people are inherently evil, or do evil things as a matter of principle. I believe people make mistakes and are re-sponsible for them. This means that when people say they are unhappy about a law, for example, they usually mean it and are not doing so to get a pay-off (although it does happen).

7. It is possible for human society to change for the better. This is not an outgrowth of the third point above, but a fact of present civilization. Stop and think about it for a moment—look how well off most of us live: central heating, indoor plumbing, food, dentistry, airplanes, smartphones, etc. A key point under-

girding my brief essays is that we can get better, and we do, but only after bumps along the way. In the main, I am an optimist.

Greece will survive and will likely continue to be a member of the European Union and the Eurozone. I hope Europe will get beyond the mistrust and see the value of retaining Greece as part of the European family. This is not a prediction, rather it is a desired outcome.

Nations go through difficult phases just like states such as California and Florida in the U.S., but no one talks about jettisoning them from the federal union. What Europe discovered is something known to us Americans, namely, that a single currency may need a strong central bank to back it up. Right now in Europe, there is a single currency, the euro, but the European Central Bank (ECB) must consider situations in various countries and is not as easily able to take measures to adjust the economy of the continent as our Federal Reserve does for the U.S.

What the Greek economic crisis has exposed is two-fold: the old business ways of Greece cannot continue (the monopolies and cartels, the rapacious middlemen, the tax evasion, the closed professions, etc.) while Europe itself has to get on better footing. It needs a strong central bank to regulate the European economy and avoid the pitfalls that have occurred since 2010.

To make these changes requires a lot of political leadership in Europe. And that's where the problem starts. It's been easy so far to blame the Greeks for their economic mismanagement, and there's a lot to be said about this, but that the buck stops in Brussels, headquarters of the E.U., has been more difficult to swallow.

If it were only Greece, then, yes, let's remove the country from the Eurozone. But it's not. Greece just brought the problem to the fore; now Europe must solve it. Should Greece be thanked for this step? I doubt it. Not when so many Greeks have lost their jobs and their livelihoods. It's a mess.

But the good news is that things will get better.

2012

Athens Burning? No Barbecues, Please!

Seattle, February 13

The images of the Starbucks burning in Athens is sad, not least of which is that this kind of destruction is unnecessary and does nothing for the image of Greece. I am also being sentimental, because it also happens to be the Starbucks where I first met my wife!

Sentiment aside, it's simply inexcusable that such a beautiful city regularly falls under the thuggery of the same group of anarchists, the same nihilists who see beauty in destruction and ugliness in every corner of globalization. Is this the best they can do to help life improve in Greece—burn it down completely? I worry about Greece, I worry about the folks who have to pay for this senseless destruction.

Greece Saved? Drama Continues!

Seattle, February 24

Last week Greece received a €100 billion ($140 billion) bailout funding from the European Union and International Monetary Fund, but at a great, great cost. In return for this money, which is badly needed by the Greek government, Greece has relinquished some of its sovereignty and indebted itself for many years. Meanwhile, worker salaries will continue to go down, and the economy will shrink further (last year it shrank by 7%).

This has no real significance for us in the U.S., but if one is in any way connected to Greece, there is much to worry about. Was there a choice? Probably not, but it does put Greece in a position where it will be trying to dig itself out of a hole for perhaps three decades. Not something to look forward to. For myself as a

Greek-born American, it's sad to see the situation unfold in Greece—its history is filled with tragedy and suffering, and this latest chapter simply adds to a long and painful tome.

Greece—A Never Ending Story

Seattle, February 28

The second bailout of Greece as well as Standard & Poor's recent downgrading of Greece's long-term credit rating to "selective default" brings to temporary conclusion that which has built up for the past two years. Greece is bankrupt and this latest S&P salvo only reinforces this reality. Of bigger concern is what happens now. Where does this little nation with thousands of years of history go now?

We know she is selling her architectural treasures, such as the Acropolis, to photographers and filmmakers, but less obvious is the exodus of many Greeks away from the cities and to family homes in the villages. It helps that Greece is a nation of mostly homeowners—80% of its residents own their own houses.

This movement may help to reinvigorate the nation—a giant back-to-the-earth phenomenon that may change the social dynamics of the country, as well as promote more produce. Don't be surprised if in a few years you see more Greek products stocked up in your local grocery store.

Renewable Energy in Greece

Seattle, March 1

We hear of the grim reality in Greece—unemployment above 21%, increase in suicides, food kitchens swamped by new entrants—and the picture that emerges is hardly pretty. Some compare the current state of Greece to the horrible years of World

War II and the Civil War that followed.

We fail to remember that since 1981, when Greece joined the European Union, its per capita income has risen six-fold. Yes, there is a severe recession in Greece, but we need to recall how different Greece is now than say thirty years ago.

Other efforts are being made to get the country back on its feet. Russia is looking for energy projects in Greece, and China is becoming more involved in the Greek economy (buying up the port of Piraeus, for example, and sending more tourists there).

And renewable energy is targeted by the government as a growth area with the help, ironically enough, of Germany. Things are bad in Greece, no doubt, but there is potential. Expect to see more wind farms and solar panels spread across the landscape in a country with 300 days of sunny weather.

Stork Brings Elections to Greece

Seattle, March 2

New parliamentary elections will take place on Sunday, April 29, 2012 to elect a new prime minister. In Greece, like in many parliamentary democracies, the prime minister of the country is the head of the political party with the most winning candidates in the election.

There is the possibility that the winning party may not have enough members of Parliament selected to form a government without support from smaller parties. The new prime minister would therefore lack a mandate to rule with confidence and vigor, but it also forces parties to collaborate in a political reality where they normally do not. So it may be a good thing, painful as it may be for politicians forced to cooperate with each other. I still believe that Greece will get out of this muddle, but it will require some soul-changing along the way.

Greece—the New Energy Hub?

Seattle, March 6

It scarcely seems possible that in the midst of all the harsh economic news for Greece, there is a potential silver lining. It has to do with possible huge deposits of oil and natural gas in the Ionian Sea and below southern Crete. If the speculation proves right, this is a game changer—not only in terms of the economic benefits to Greece, but to the energy needs of Europe.

Later this month the Ministry of the Environment (headed by former Finance Minister Giorgos Papaconstantinou) is slated to sign energy cooperation agreements with Cyprus and Israel to boost further exploration of these deposits. It will certainly add a new wrinkle to the image of Greece, and help reduce her (as well as Europe's) dependence on Middle East oil.

Greece Gets New Life Lease—For Now!

Seattle, March 8

The majority acceptance of bondholders of the new debt deal offered by the Greek government raises hopes that for the moment the economic crisis is abating, while unemployment inches upwards and further pension cuts take their toll on an already battered economy.

Some economic analysts still predict an outright Greek debt default and an exit from the Eurozone, but for the moment that seems far away. The attention paid to Greece in the past few months—both by global stock markets as well as in the news— shows the extent to which worries about the country's economic collapse have on Europe.

Many in Greece do not want the attention, but it has forced many others to examine their role in how the country is operated. I suspect that Greece may be a different country in a few years;

with a smaller government and a more export-savvy economy. For tourists, this is an excellent time to visit the country!

A Greek Spring?

Seattle, March 11

Last year's Arab Spring sent shockwaves around the Middle East and North Africa; popular uprisings toppled the dictators of Tunisia, Libya, and Egypt, and drastically reordered the political landscape of the area. It is possible that Syria, for far more complicated reasons, may be next.

In Greece, there is no such revolution, but the new elections for prime minister this spring may herald a new era in the political environment of Greece. Antonis Samaras, head of the conservative New Democracy, looks set to win the race, although whether he will do so alone or as part of a coalition is too early to tell.

Samaras does not come from a famous political family (e.g., Papandreou, Caramanlis, Bakoyannis, etc.), so he brings a certain "freshness" to the table. Questions remain, however: Will he be able to substantially change the political culture of Greece and rid it of corruption, clientelism, favoritism, and an overbearing state bureaucracy that stifles innovation?

The challenges in Greece seem insurmountable, but any effective leader with a desire for reform in Greece would get noticeable support from a weary public exhausted from years of social and political injustice. If ever a "spring" was needed, it is in Greece.

Greece—Under Construction

Seattle, March 12

What does a society look like when it's being transformed? We know it's hard for an individual to change; imagine an entire nation going through this process. Yet Greece is forced to do exactly that. We read the stories of personal angst in Greece: more homelessness, rising unemployment, families in deep pain.

Less common are the stories of perseverance and social solidarity. I leave for Greece on the 20th of this month to start a study abroad program. Along the way I will post my thoughts and observations about the nation and its transformation. There are stories to be told, feelings to be shared.

I suspect we will see the budding yearnings of a new country emerging from the wreckage. For my students in the study abroad program to Greece, I hope they will see the opportunity to be a part of this birthing process, and to provide some healing and comfort to a demoralized people. Just their presence alone in Greece may bring a little uplift.

Great Greek Soul

Seattle, March 14

Of the many questions I've been asked about the current economic situation in Greece, one remains—what can we do to help? It's not easy to answer. Plan a trip to Greece? Buy imported Greek products? Patronize Greek restaurants? When my students and I head out to Greece next week, we will arrive in a country that is barely recognizable from the one that only a few years ago hosted a triumphant Olympic Games.

The swagger of the people is gone, fear and worry seem a daily routine now and the future looks bleak. Yet when I think about the past in Greece, the picture brightens. The suffering of the Greek people, so beautifully and touchingly captured in their music and dance, has been a constant, whether in World War II and the tragic Civil War that followed, whether in the economic collapse of the 1890s, the brutal independence struggle of the 1830s, or even the tragedy of the 1922 Smyrna disaster.

Yet somehow, the Greek soul emerges intact. Somehow. I asked my students going to Northern Greece to reflect on this a bit—to see how Greeks cope with challenges and learn from this process. Greeks tend to turn disaster into culture, and this offers us travelers a chance to see something unique. This really is a special time to go to Greece, to watch this process in action. And to learn how to cope with our own tragedies, which invariably come.

As a Greek-born American, I am not proud of how this country has fallen from its nebulous perch just a few years ago, but I am very aware that a new nation is being built, and we live through history in seeing it take place before our eyes. That is why we go to Greece. And that is how anyone can help make this transformed country one that generations will be proud to be a part of.

Birthing a New Nation, Part 1—Local Produce

Seattle, March 16

Here are the statistics: Last year, Greece imported 15,550 tons of tomatoes, 29,485 tons of lemons, 22,704 tons of apples, 174,352 tons of potatoes, 102,036 tons of beef, and 194,281 tons of pork.

This from a nation that grows and raises all these foodstuffs. The culprit? Greeks desire for fresh fruit, vegetables and meat all year round. Rather than being satisfied with seasonal fruits and vegetables, residents in Greece want their foodstuff—and they want it now.

With the economic crisis at hand, this looks increasingly like a luxury. So what are Greeks doing about it? The movement for farmers to sell directly to consumers, removing the costly middlemen (they are usually men and not women!), grows. This direct-to-consumer marketing is done online as well.

Organic farming is also getting a boost; local farmers' markets that are long a mainstay of Greek social life are emerging as quality alternatives to supermarkets. In Athens, such markets seem to be increasing, at least so far as I observed. As this phenomenon spreads to other parts of Greece, it shows the human spirit is alive and well in Greece.

Greek Necessity the Mother of Invention

Seattle, March 18

A British reporter goes around Greece to see how folks there are coping with the country's economic malaise. He discusses how a theater company in Thessaloniki in Northern Greece is accepting food for tickets to watch a theater production. The food is distributed to those in need. Sound desperate? Perhaps, but it's a novel way for the theater company to attract audiences and to help out during a time of great difficulty.

Sure, it's a publicity stunt (publicity is the lifeblood of the arts!), but it is also creative and compelling. How does an actor, for example, survive in an economic crisis? How does she perform when the unemployment rate is near depression levels? In a previous entry, I wrote about the direct-to-consumer selling of produce. It's now called the "Potato Movement."

There is an interesting story told by writer Elie Wiesel about a group of rabbis in a concentration camp in Germany during World War II who decide to put God on trial for the events of that horrible war. At the end of this trial God is found guilty of "crimes against humanity." But after the guilty verdict is read, the rabbis leave to go to prayer. How do we deal with difficulty? Sometimes folk wisdom hits the nail on the head: the true captain of a boat is revealed in a storm, not in a calm sea!

Greece Welcomes Another Venizelos!

Seattle, March 19

He is not related to the great Eleftherios Venizelos (aka Athens International Airport), Greece's most eminent Prime Minister and great national modernizer in the early 1900s, but Evangelos Venizelos carries the all-important brand name. It's like a politician in the U.S. named Washington or Lincoln. Schooled in France and a constitutional lawyer by training, this heavy-rock-singer Steve Grimmett look-alike could have easily played a heavy in any Frank Capra movie. Mr. Potter in *It's a Wonderful Life* comes easily to mind.

But can he lead Greece? Over the weekend, in a resounding turnout of 236,151 PASOK party members and voters, Venizelos got 97% of the vote as the new party head. He ran unopposed. As a result, today he resigned his post as Minister of Finance. He returned the favor by calling the European Union "colorless, conservative, and slow to react" to the great economic crisis in Greece. So much for European unity.

Venizelos once was rumored to be having an extra-marital affair; when his father-in-law found out, he arranged for some thugs to give Venizelos a good whipping. Elections for prime minster are coming in April or early May. Whether he is prepared to lead Greece during one of its worst crises in its modern history remains to be seen. But we can all rest assured knowing he won't cheat on his wife.

Mandarin Spring of Greece

Athens, March 21

Returning to Athens, after last being here in September 2011, I observed an eerie quality to human faces and buildings in this ancient city. Shell-shocked folks in their peculiarly dark, winter clothing, walked past rows of empty storefronts and lifeless buildings covered in chaotic graffiti.

The weather is pleasant enough for someone coming from Seattle and its cold rain. But at the airport here, no line formed for taxis, where once the queue was horrendously long.

During the Athens 2004 Olympic Games, the airport was literally a zoo, but was now hauntingly and utterly silent except for announcements of where passengers could pick up their luggage.

It is March to be sure, and the tourists have not yet arrived, but there's a palatable somberness to this city. The plane from Amsterdam was hardly full (interestingly, the first class section near empty!), and KLM just announced it will reduce service between Athens and Amsterdam this year.

But there is one sign of Athens that doesn't change, that in a way describes its character—its thousands of planted mandarin trees. No one in Athens seems to know when these trees were planted, but they are now in full bloom with ripened mandarins too bitter and pungent to eat.

And once ripened, they fall on cars, on sidewalks, on people... and are left to rot. Apparently, these trees were originally planted because they are hearty and can withstand the city smog, yet all that planting has now become rotting fruit on the sidewalks and streets. Perhaps they could be picked and turned into something—compost for gardens comes to mind. There are also planted olive trees along the sidewalks, but I don't think anyone picks their fruit either.

Yet each year, no matter the weather or other conditions, these mandarin trees bear fruit. Just like the Greeks themselves.

Greek Shock of the New

Athens, March 22

The first day being back in Athens revealed differences from my last stay in September 2011. The shock of seeing some of my favorite haunts closed hit me hard; the favorite old bookstore, gone; the favorite new bookstore, gone; the favorite newspaper stand, gone; my favorite shoe store, gone.

It was like coming to an old Hollywood back-lot, empty, when the filming had long gone and the wind kicked up the lonely dust. This was not the Plaka in downtown Athens, where the Acropolis is located, that I remembered, I cherished. It's a graying version, like a favorite uncle who's suffered a mild stroke and can't walk very well anymore. You feel pity but realize there's nothing you can do except hold onto the memories.

I once feared this Plaka; it seemed like a privileged place for only tough-minded Athenians. But after only my first stay here more than twenty years ago, it felt like home; a village within a larger city. Coming from a tiny hamlet on the Greek island of Euboea, I appreciated and responded to this feeling.

Soon I was talking to the locals: Tom the crazy Irish artist by way of Israel and Palestine; Kyria Anna at her little café across from the New Acropolis Museum; Kyria Christina and her eponymous bakery and her sage advice never to marry (marriage is for idiots, she once warned me!) and the older gent (he can't be more than four-and-a-half feet tall) who shines my shoes near Syntagma Square. My "homies" who recognize me each time I return to this city (my honorarium: "Kyrie Kathigitai"—"Mister Professor") and seem happy to see me. This is my hood, my alternate home, my cherished place of refuge.

Now, well, they all seem a bit sadder, hung-shouldered, a bit weary around the eyes. Their smiles may be the same (Greeks must have some of the nicest teeth in the world!), but underneath them rests weariness and resignation. Everywhere, everywhere—on lips, in blank gazes, in slow trudging steps—are the traces of the "troubles" that have settled on this beautiful landscape. I dreaded seeing all this, going on this walk the first day I arrived, knowing how it would hit me, but all the same I had to do it; I had to see with my own eyes the results of the economic malaise.

As I completed my tour of the Plaka, absorbing the sad sights, I was surprised to find in the midst of the ashes some tiny phoenixes rising. At 30 Nikis Street, the sight of a former Fair Trade shop is a new vegetarian restaurant ("Avocado") brimming with business.

Around the corner, and across from where the former Compendium used bookstore resided, in a spot once occupied by a very nasty and overbearing travel agent, is a cute upscale café designed for the young and urban and trendy.

And sitting in it were the beautiful people; I don't know of another country that has produced so many attractive men and women, a veritable factory of the excessively comely. They sat grinning and smoking, posing really, in their thick-soled pumps (noticeably, last year's models; the economy's affecting them too!), escapees from a Quentin Tarantino movie. Things may be bad, but in Greece, there's always an attractive face smiling.

For a Fistful of Gyros

Athens, March 23

He came rushing to me right after I just got my hot-wrapped gyro at my favorite stand just outside the Athens metro station

Syngrou Fix. I was starving, but so apparently was he. He asked me something, I wasn't sure in what language it was, then came the Greek word for "hunger"—"pinao"—and he even threw me a couple of words in Italian.

It was a quick moment, as such encounters go, but it is at such moments that life's struggles—tectonic moral struggles—take place. I was not prepared for it. The encounter, as brief as it was, haunted me all night.

Should I have given him some of my gyro? Or what about the candy that I keep in my pocket just for such a purpose? What obligation do we have to those apparently less fortunate than we? Or by giving in to the begging, do we simply perpetuate it without any salvation, or hope that the problem will vanish?

Such encounters took place in Greece even before the economic crisis; it is a fact of European life that begging is a common sight. The Roma people (usually referred to as "Gypsies") originated from India and are usually associated with such activity (women holding babies, sometimes directly in the sunlight, squatting on sidewalks), but begging cuts across all ethnic groups.

Once outside a church in the Athenian suburb of Holargos, my wife and I observed a Roma family near the church steps. The father and mother, both seemingly in their twenties, were begging for money from churchgoers, while their two children—a boy of about 8-9 and a girl of around 11-12—played nearby. I observed the girl suddenly take on the role of an old lady, begging, as if it was a game. And surely it was. Someday it might be real. And hence the awful stereotype that stigmatizes this ethnic group.

I keep candy in my pocket for just such encounters. But I also feel that this is simply a cop-out on my part. As it is, I think, for all of us who give in these kinds of situations.

A better approach might be to simply stop and try to learn something about the person, which I know would surely frighten the beggar.

It's an easy exchange—someone begs me for money, and I respond—but a tougher exchange would be for me to understand the culture of the beggar, to understand this person as a human being. That requires something on both our parts—something more deliberate and sincere. The exchange of money is so emblematic of our commercial age—it has no real value and certainly nothing humane. But it does assuage our guilt for a bit, and let's us go our merry way to dream bigger dreams.

Meaning of Goodness

Athens, March 24

It began in the Monasteraki area of the Plaka, a ramshackle collection of 19th century buildings housing various knick-knack shops—tourist meccas for the bargain minded. I came to repair the shoulder bag my wife bought for me last September.

I found the shop, saw the owner, and showed him the broken buckle on my shoulder strap. As he was repairing it, I looked at wallets—I needed a wallet to carry my money but also another little wallet to carry my loose change (common in the old days, rarely seen today). Instead of buying the model I had before, I decided to try a new model, less expensive. I saved two euros. I was a rich man.

Feeling proud of my penuriousness, I resumed my tasks for the day—picking up students at the airport. It's a delight to go to the airport and see my students beaming with excitement at coming to Greece—they keep the rest of the world slightly less cynical than Greece would be otherwise.

On the way back to downtown Athens from the airport, I got off at the Syngrou Fix metro station, two students in tow. I decided to stop at a kiosk ("periptero") to buy them water—I know they were thirsty because I surely was. As I reached into the fridge to grab the three bottles of water, I had my new little change purse open—and change suddenly scattered on a stack of newspapers. A 2-euro coin hung on the edge of one newspaper. When I reached for it, it fell through my fingers and disappeared. I searched in vain to find it.

Two older gents stood around me, watching me with a mixture of disgust and curiosity. If I wasn't stupid once, I was stupid twice—again reaching into the fridge to grab another bottle of water and again more change fell from my new purse.

I tapped on the window of the kiosk, telling the proprietor that loose change had fallen in his pile of newspapers. He shrugged, as all Greeks typically do, adding, "And what do you want me to do about it?" It's something of a national saying, this. I didn't know exactly what he should do, but there's a little loadfull of change somewhere in his newspapers. I felt stupid and foolish, but mustered whatever shred of dignity I had left and simply walked away. Sometimes in life one loses, and the more one tries to get out of it, the further the losses rise.

Long ago I learned to fight such daily indignities with the only weapon I had—blast the world around me with love. Four American students heading to the airport wondered if they had to go another stop; I walked by and told them this was their exit.

Then another man, as I was returning from the airport with another student, asked me if the train was headed for downtown Athens. It was, I told him. He sat next to the student. What stop was he getting off? Akropoli.

"Great. That's on the way to our stop. I'll tell you when to get off." And I did, even giving him some tips on where to eat near his hotel, what places to avoid, and where to visit. My stupidity was soon forgotten. I was a member of the human race again.

Crisis? Greek Life Goes On!

Athens, March 25

Syntagma Square is a landmark symbol to Greeks. This is where, in the 19th century, Greeks fed up with a constitutional monarchy demanded a democratic constitution—and got one. Hence, the name. ("Syntagma" in Greek means "Constitution.") In the early 1900s, it was a haven for cafés, a mini-version of the Champs-Elysees.

Since then, it has been paved over by marble and is a scene to rendezvous, people watch, hawk bread sticks and lottery tickets, and gather to protest when strikes are called.

In other words, your typical downtown commons. It is a human ping-pong machine. The high and the low mix here in odd and sometimes poetic ways. The beautiful people always make an appearance or two—men in their tight T-shirts and greased punk hair and women in their jeans and ballet-flats, walking with studied surliness as if cameras were taking photos.

To come to Syntagma is to witness the unexpected. I encountered the Indignado Movement in June 2011 only to be told by one crazed denizen of the encampment that I was surely a police spy. He cornered me and told me to confess my transgression. When I assured him I was not a police informer but rather an academic, he laughed and shouted for all to hear that I was a police informer. It was time to leave, I reckoned.

Today, the Indignado movement is part of history, just another small blip in the history of this Square. People-watching is back, but the unexpected continues as always. Today as I was heading for some shopping, there was a military band smack dab in the middle of the Square playing "Rolling On the River," which is a little like a band playing "Zorba the Greek" in the middle of New Orleans.

And then it was sunset, or "magic hour" in filmmaking talk,

where in the soft, orange light of the setting sun, faces take on an ethereal look. The man waited; a Russian-looking man in an elegant suit and the usual European pointed shoes.

The attractive woman in high heels ran to him. They met and hugged, and kissed, hugged and kissed, hugged . . . Oblivious to everyone around them, they were entranced in themselves, following another rhythm than the one around them. It's hard not to get a bit sentimental watching this. And this too is part of Syntagma.

Rebuilding a Nation: Barcodes

Athens, March 26

Greeks, like many of us since the worldwide economic crisis hit in 2008, have received a lesson in how capitalism works. Like many, I was vaguely aware of Credit Default Swaps prior to this period; now, bond yields, haircuts, and "credit events" are part of our vocabulary.

You can now add "barcodes" to that growing list. It began with the Potato Movement in Greece, and it spread to a "Buy Greek" phenomenon that only seems to grow.

How can you help Greece? Look for products with the barcodes that begin with the number 520 or 521. I got a civics lesson about this recently. After reading about Greek barcodes in *Athens News*, I did some shopping in Athens to find out the state of manufacturing in the country. Would it be difficult to find products produced in Greece or by companies based in Greece as the barcode suggests? I was surprised to find that there are more products made in Greece than I realized. I bought a baseball cap for two euros. Made in Greece. Nail clips, files, scissors—all made in Greece at inexpensive prices. And this was just the tip of the iceberg. Local residents are demanding to buy fruits and vegetables grown in the country. This is heralded in the local media in almost messianic if not revolutionary terms. The benefits seem enormous: reducing energy costs from bringing in produce from other countries (e.g., lemons from Argentina) and helping local farmers at the same time.

Lemons from Argentina? Greece has been a lemon paradise for many years, but during the go-go years of the 2000s, it was more chic to buy foreign. No longer.

What real effect this has on the Greek economy is hard to measure. Yet when hundreds of thousands of city residents are considering moving to the countryside to become farmers, it no longer seems just a cute fad. It's back-to-basics time in Greece. The celebrity culture that threatened to turn work into a four-letter word seems less vital these days. All because of three numbers on a barcode.

Neighborhood Bench for Social News

Athens, March 27

The bench in the tiny park near the Art Gallery Hotel by the Acropolis serves as a rest-stop for many local residents. It is a gathering place for locals, mostly retirees. I find myself taking to this bench as a rest-stop, but also to catch up with the local gossip.

One day I was eating my gyro when an elderly woman, in her 70s, asked me if she could join me on the bench. I said, of course, and she sat down next to me.

She complained that life is changing in Greece. I asked how so. She said the other day she saw a woman of some means go to the "laiki" (farmer's market) up the street, and after it closed, the woman pulled her scarf over her face and proceeded to rummage through the garbage bins of left-over produce for food.

The elderly woman continued: "I saw her the other day and asked her about it. The woman claimed she didn't know what I was talking about. I asked her, 'Why are you lying?' The elderly woman shook her head plaintively. "Things are bad and getting worse."

"Is this as bad as in the Second World War?" I asked. "No," she replied. Rather, it reminded her of 1956. "An awful time." She mentioned "the dictatorship," and I wondered if she was confusing it with the time of the Colonels, 1967 to 1974.

In my mind, I was thinking of following up on this comment but remained silent. Looking back now, I wish I had asked her about this particular year. And why did the word "dictatorship" ("thithaktoria") come to mind? Where was she going with this comment?

The wounds of the past schism between the left and the right that was sown at the founding of an independent Greece in 1830 have never really healed. They exploded with vicious fury during World War II and the Greek Civil War that followed; the poisoned residue of this internal conflict rages under the surface today.

One hopes that, on the last day of caretaker Prime Minister Lucas Papademos's term, he addresses the nation in an attempt to heal itself from this internal strife. If so, that moment alone would go a long way towards national recovery for this tiny country.

Across from us, the kiosk that I had frequented in past visits was shuttered, and the produce stand in front of us was sparsely stocked—not the bountiful produce I remembered from previous years. The woman's words seemed intensified by this reality. A pitiful moment, her sad tale, but one strangely familiar to me. I've heard tales of woe before; it seems part of the Greek gene. It felt to me like the anguish of the perennial state of Greece—always in disarray, always something to complain about. Scenes like this at a neighborhood bench seem to me a way to vent and spew the pain of life to anyone who will listen. I don't believe this is a sunk people for a moment, but it's hard not to feel sadness and heartache when hearing these tales of woe.

What will such stories do to the fabric of this neighborhood?

The Old and New of Greece

Ioannina, March 27

The bus ride from Athens to Ioannina offers glimpses of the future and the past of Greece. Heading northwest, it heads towards Corinth then turns north towards Patras.

The stretch of this national highway is unfinished; half-built bridges lie rusting in the spring sun, even a concrete mixing truck sits dormant on a work site. It's as if an invasion from Mars scattered all the construction workers in the middle of a shift.

Orange cones and construction barriers line long stretches of the road, true of the past two years. Will it ever be finished? One wonders.

But it makes navigating through this maze of unfinished business tortuous. There is the stunning scenery to soothe the troubled soul—and I do mean stunning. Many times have I traversed this highway, and each time my breath fails me—the shimmering water, the sense of lazy peace and tranquility are almost unbearable to watch, otherworldly.

Behind the highway, to your left as you speed ahead, are mountains that in another world would be backdrops to a western movie; crag-like terrain, large buttes, huge crevices that seem clawed by nature.

The ride would not be complete without the human element. This is Greece, after all, and one is never too far from the human touch. Immediately upon entering the bus in Athens, the driver welcomed everyone aboard in a loud voice and said that if there was anything he could do for us, to let him know. This was the first time I had ever experienced such hospitality on a bus. Was the economic crisis making everyone nicer?

Mid-way on the Corinth-Patras Highway, he pulled over to a McDonald's on the side of the road, evidently to pick up a passenger. But he drove on when there was no sign of anyone. Then, some distance ahead, the driver suddenly pulled over after honking his horn (very loudly!) for some seconds. He stopped on the edge of an off-ramp, jumped out of the bus, and shouted to people inside a black Mercedes—asking them why they didn't stop at the McDonald's.

The driver came back onto the bus and asked all of us—"Did I not stop back there to pick up the passenger?" He needed witnesses, but many were barely awake. Those that were, nodded fiercely. "See, good thing I have witnesses," and he went outside, and resumed his yelling at the Mercedes. Eventually, after a few minutes, a meek-looking female passenger got on the bus, paid her ticket, and sat quietly in her seat. A few minutes later, the whole scene was forgotten.

We crossed the Rio Antirio bridge, a relatively new suspension bridge that seemed ethereally new—almost Disneyish new. It connects Peloponnesos with the mainland in spectacular fashion. Crossing it is like stepping into the 22nd century. Once on the other side, the old resumes. A reminder, perhaps, that this nation is burdened by its past—that the old is never just old, but alive. And moving into a new era thus becomes difficult.

As we neared Ioannina, the old was visible in not just the buildings and the sheep in the fields, but in the sense that the country is perennially under construction—that the new IKEA store competes with houses that belong to the 19th century. We arrived at our bus stop and got off on the side of the highway. The University of Ioannina campus lay ahead. Its new buildings gleamed in the sun, but the graffiti on them made them seem old.

The Great Greek Migration

Ioannina, March 28

Under its title of "Greeks drawn by village life," *Kathimerini* reveals the astonishing figure that 70% of Greek respondents are thinking of moving away from the city to the country for a better quality life. About 20% have already started making preparations.

This goes against the grain of urban trends. For the past few hundred years, the shift has been from rural to urban. In the United States, it was in 1924 that the urban population of the country overtook its rural population. That same feat on a global scale was accomplished in 2007. Now Greeks are reversing this migration.

It is possible that of those 70% only a few will actually make the move. It is not easy to switch from a city to a village. Such polls are only snapshots of people's thinking, not their actions, and perhaps capture something of their weariness and economic desperation.

But as astonishing as it seems, there may be something real to this movement. Many of the 70% simply want a quieter, less stressful life, even if it comes with lower income. They may also be tired of the career ladder-climbing that invariably demands so much out of young professionals. And no one can beat the fresh air and charm of the countryside.

If the economic crisis continues much longer, it is feasible that many will indeed migrate out of the city into the rural villages. If the crisis passes, the desire for such a move may wither. Time will surely tell. Meanwhile, such a phenomenon represents a field day for sociologists and budding sociologists. I can already see the dissertation proposals being written!

The Poetic Soul of Greece

Ioannina, March 28

On World Poetry Day, they protested by holding up banners with quotes from famous Greek poets. They gathered in Syntagma Square on Wednesday, March 21, 2012. Greece has seen so many demonstrations—from the absurd to the violent—but nothing quite like this.

There was a sign by a middle-aged woman showing a quote by Odysseus Elytis: "If you cannot find spring, make it." Another read: "I call upon you, art of poetry."

World Poetry Day is an annual event initiated by Unesco; it was not intended to cause any protest, but somehow it was fitting: Poets, long being rebels of society, used to denounce the austerity measures imposed on Greece by its foreign creditors. It is easy to dismiss this event as a publicity gimmick, but quaint as it might seem, poetry at its best is a way to crash through the cant and banality of life, so as to paint a new way of living.

We don't really read poetry any more, and our lives are the poorer for it. We don't see it as wisdom, pleasure, or reflection. We see poetry a little like those old rotary phones—best left for the museums. Or in this case, in academia, where only a few egg-heads, cut off from reality and common sense, read poetry as if it were part of some ancient religious cult.

None of this does justice to the power, the true power of words. Think about it: the majesty of life boiled down to mere words that spark beauty, thought, and knowledge little captured by any other art. Poetry has haunted my life. I wrote some poems when I was young, and they were wretched, but it taught me to appreciate poetry when it is grandly done.

It is a sad truth that a poetry protest would never take place in America; it would cause people to laugh themselves silly. But, in Greece, where words still matter, where how they are nailed to-

45

gether can say a lot about the quality of one's life and one's being, well . . . such a protest deserves our respect. It's a moving tribute in a world where we rarely boast of any emotion around mere words.

New "Energy Axis" for Greece-Cyprus-Israel

Ioannina, March 29

Today's *Kathimerini* reveals the emerging new energy hub in the eastern Mediterranean Sea as a result of discoveries of massive new oil and natural gas deposits. This upends the geopolitical scene in the region.

For some years, it has been known that there were deposits near and around Cyprus and Crete, but previous Greek governments refused to conduct further research in the area for fear of antagonizing Turkey.

With Greece in desperate economic crisis and relations between Turkey and Israel in disarray, the time seemed ripe to finally explore these sites. How the exploration will change the dynamics between Greece and Turkey seems too early to tell, but tensions between the two nations may increase. Ironically, this comes at a time when trade between the two countries rises. Turkey is the third leading market for Greek goods, and Turkish businesses seek opportunities to expand trade into Greece.

It is hard to imagine Greece being an exporter of energy; this will certainly change perceptions of the country, both within and outside its borders. For Greece, long dependent on imports to sustain its economy—from oil to grain—this brightens her economic outlook. For outsiders, Greece may become more than just another pretty place to visit—but one also worth investing in.

Missing from the discussion is the environmental impact of oil and natural gas drilling. If Greece is known mostly for her astounding beauty, then what will happen if there is an oil spill?

What about the impact of increased shipping on delicate coral reefs that brighten her shorelines? These issues are not raised in media reports on the drilling, and answers may take time. Meanwhile, as the excitement about this new "Energy Axis" builds, the flagging morale of an entire nation may change.

Squeezing Pain into Greek Culture

Ioannina, March 29

As strange as it sounds, the process of how culture is formed reminds me of how we produced olive oil in the village of my youth. It involved a stone press and a donkey going around in circles for hours. The single olive was crushed, and out of it poured oil, producing a foul smell in the process. Today, this is done by machines, and foul odors are eliminated.

Today's pain in Greece may be tomorrow's song, dance, movie, story or poem. But it will take a while; it will not come suddenly. The pain must seep into people's bones, wrangle around with their souls and then, one day, magically, like the oil pouring out of the squeezed olive, emerge as culture.

We don't wish tragedy on anyone; to do so is to want to inflict pain. This cannot be so. But we can say that once tragedy arrives, the trick is to see it not as an end, but a means to a better end.

When that moment comes, the pain will have subsided, and the country will be on better footing. Then onto the next challenge, and thus does life go in circles. And also advances. It is hard to think of renewal and potential progress in the midst of pain.

I react strongly to the chanting in a Greek Orthodox Church—it seems to me that that melodic and haunting chanting captures the tragedy and pain of Greek life. It is as if the chanting comes from some deep bowel within the earth, a pit where all the human suffering is stored and lies stacked one on top of each other.

Perhaps this pain simply connects us to our humanity. It is hard to be arrogant when aware of such pain.

Rebuilding a Nation: New Social Contract

Ioannina, March 30

What is our relationship to our government? Do we trust it? Does it look after our welfare and security? Should we obey it?

It's Friday here in Greece. Spring blooms. The scent of a new season blows with the gentle wind. Is this the time to be talking about governments and people?

When John Locke wrote about the social contract in 1689, he meant it as a way to support community. It's an urban concept, in some regards. Human beings come together and find that by giving up some personal rights in favor of a functioning community, greater order, peace, and security are maintained. Not to mention commerce and social advancement.

But what happens when those in government simply do not meet the needs of the community? In today's *Kathimerini* article, Greece's ombudsman, Calliope Spanou, suggests that the Greek state is not working. She offers examples of government incompetence and dysfunction: different rulings by different departments, weakened ministries, new rulings that complicate past ones, etc.

The attitude of Greek citizens does not help: the expectations that government will do everything for them. The people are not willing to accept that *they* are the government. Democracy's a bitch.

Can a new social contract be drawn in Greece? Yes. In such a crisis, anything is possible. New rules can be written. Often, this is the only (and best) time to do so.

'Good Karma' Rules of Travel

Ioannina, March 30

I have traveled for over twenty years; most of my trips have been to Greece, but I have also been to various other European nations, as well as Canada and Mexico. Besides traveling light, I follow my 'Good Karma Rules': ones that have served me well over these years.

1. Leave a tip in the hotel bathroom for the cleaning ladies (I have yet to encounter a man cleaning hotel rooms!). For me, it's one euro per day in the hotel. It's a hard job to clean up after people in hotels. I can't imagine what refuse they have seen doing this duty. I notice that when I return to the same hotel, the cleaning staff is very nice to me.

2. Be polite to everyone you meet in your travels. Stories abound of travelers who've chatted with a fellow passenger, only for the passenger to end up providing valuable help. In some rare cases, travelers have ended up marrying the fellow passenger!

3. Thank flight attendants for their professionalism. Flight attendants usually work hard to make sure you are comfortable and attended to you during flight. It's a tough job, not easy to carry out. Unless it's a terrible flight, I usually thank the flight staff on my way out of the airplane.

4. Respect local traditions. As much as we want to assume our way is better, the local way is right because you are the visitor and not the native.

5. Eating can be mediation. In North America, we tend to view food as something you shove down your throat when you are hungry. In Greece, food is a social lubricant, a way to stay connected and develop relationships with others. Even if you eat alone, you can still appreciate the life that gives us such tasty food. Reflect on that for a bit and see what you come up with.

6. Turn airports into exercise halls. If I have a layover of more than two hours, I use that time to walk around the airport to exercise my cramped legs. This is a way to respect my body; sitting in an airplane for (in my case) over ten hours, with limited time to get up and stretch my legs (mostly because of U.S. Federal regulations against congregating around bathrooms) is hard on my legs. Exercising them benefits my body; in my wanderings, I also spot any sales as well. So it comes with benefits.

7. Keep learning, keep growing. It's surprising what I can learn by keeping an open mind when I travel—being exposed to a new way of doing things, a new idea, or an interesting new trend. Keeps us growing.

8. Lastly, expect things to go wrong. Flights are delayed. Planes develop mechanical problems. Stress-free flights are rare. Professional travelers build this fact into their attitude. They learn to go with the flow. I also keep a toothbrush, toothpaste, and extra pair of briefs in my carry-on bag for that missed flight that requires an overnight stay.

Falling in Love with Northern Greece!

Ioannina, March 31

Ioannina contains about 80,000 souls and, according to Wikipedia, stands about 500 meters above sea level. It is located in the northwest corner of Greece, in a region of fierce independent types known as Epirus. The city was founded in the 6th century by Byzantine Emperor Justinian, but settlements in the area date thousands of years before.

It is charming, it is quaint, it is old, it is new. It is also a laid-back city with cute shops, great food, relaxed people, and charming cafes. It is not a place on the destination maps of most tours to Greece. The city itself has no great beaches, and many shops shutter for the afternoon nap. It almost goes out of its way to be a "non-tourist" destination. Yet, there is something lovely and noble and stately about this place.

I first came here three years ago on my first study-abroad to Ioannina. I had always done such programs in Athens; so I dreaded coming to what seemed like the backwaters of Greece. A month after arriving, I found myself drawn into its charms and quiet pace of life. And by the end of my stay in Ioannina, I had fallen in love with the place. Why?

History leaves residues on a city's buildings. Walking around the Ioannina, with its confluence of Muslim, Jewish and Christian elements, I was left pondering how this mix worked together, how it blended, how it kneaded itself into a unique place.

There is not just one history here but all different types: ancient, byzantine, modern, ethnic, religious, imperialist. Many a foreign foot has trampled its flowered hills, and somehow the place has absorbed it all. And kept its dignity; even been ennobled by it.

Our world today divides us more than blends us together. Our social media does a superb job of giving us the ability to connect to like-minded people, so we don't really tolerate diversity very much. We go for the comfortable, not the necessary. Our human relations are limited by what we like, not by what we need. We live in the gulag of our own comfort zones.

What Ioannina demands of us is an awakening to get out of our own narrow minds and to step into a different, more enlightened way of thinking. Perhaps it is to live as this city once did (and in some small ways still does!)—in a rich milieu of difference and cultural diversity.

That is why I fell in love with Ioannina.

Working for the Banks!

Ioannina, March 31

If you were bankrupt, how would you get out of it? Sell all you could? Get an extra job? Move into a cheap living situation? Countries are no different when it comes to this issue. In the case of Greece, this involves selling state assets.

Many European countries own significant amounts of shares in private companies, often involving power, energy, transportation, or, in the case of Greece, gambling. This may seem unusual in neo-liberal nations like the U.S. where government is not a shareholder of private companies (except for the auto companies it bought during the depth of the economic meltdown in 2008), yet Europeans have no such social stigma associated with it.

The company shares that Greece plans to sell to private holders are worth a fraction of their pre-crisis levels. The country needs the money but this is the wrong time to sell anything in Greece—the price returns are unbelievably low. Bargain hunters salivate at this opportunity. They can buy successful gambling company OPAP (Greeks are notoriously addicted gamblers!) as well oil refiner Hellenic Petroleum. Such bargains do not come any cheaper, and this transfer of wealth from Greece to outside investors leaves the country as a rented society. Profits go elsewhere.

Further, because of the recent Private Sector Involvement (PSI) agreement in which bondholders took a 70% haircut or write-down, Greece is obligated to pay back her loans—and make no investments in education, social welfare or infrastructure. In effect, the citizens of Greece—through taxes—are working for the country's bondholders. And this makes the citizens very angry. Can this anger be channeled into positive change for the nation?

Day Rich, Long

Ioannina, April 1

Ioannina on a weekend seems pleasantly peaceful; in a city already slow-paced, weekends are even slower than normal.

The richness of the city comes in its people and the interesting encounters possible with them. When I left my shoe shopping expedition, I found myself sitting on a bench. Next to me, a blonde street cleaning woman was talking into her mobile. After her conversation, she turned to me, looking at my backpack. "Going hiking on a mountain?"

I regarded her, taken by surprise. "No, it's just to carry stuff."

"People do that these days."

"How are things going for you?" I asked her.

"I work for the city. Things are . . ." But she stopped and just left it hanging. I could fill in the blank myself.

Later, I found myself walking by a church. Outside, as I always remember it, was a woman with two children, begging. I always seem to see her sitting on the top-most step of the church entrance. This time, the priest was there, offering them bread and giving one of the kids money. They had a relationship.

I was curious about when the church had its mass. I looked at the schedule. It said 7 A.M., but that seemed early to me.

Going inside, an older woman saw me and approached me. Perhaps she worked there, I was not sure, but I asked her anyway: "What time does service start on Sundays?"

She regarded me oddly. "In the morning."

"What time in the morning?"

"In the morning," she repeated, as if talking to a child. And with that she walked away.

It's a different concept of time here. Life is not ordered (controlled? demanded? hemmed in?) by clocks, but by simple parameters. Come in the morning. What was morning? I decide.

The church would be there, possibly the service still going on.

The day in Ioannina is as rich as it is long.

Rebuilding a Nation: Marketing Greek Food

Ioannina, April 1

The "Lex Column" in the *Financial Times* was very clear about it: Greece has assets on which it can rebuild itself. One of them is its reputation for excellent cuisine. It is one of the main attractions for many visitors.

Yet it seems that it has not really taken advantage of this reality. It ships 60% of its olive oil in bulk to the Italians, who in turn package it and reap the benefits of higher markup prices. Grocery stores in the U.S. stock Greek feta, but they also stock the cheese from France as well. Greece commands just 28% of the worldwide feta market. How did Greece get out-maneuvered on its own natural turf?

Packaging, design, and exporting Greek products is not considered "sexy." For many Greeks, I think products like olive oil and feta cheese remind them of the country's agricultural roots. People today get excited by the latest iPad, not the current brand of processed figs.

It's a narrow-minded view in many ways; it is also economically short-sighted. The iPad or any other piece of new technology employs factory workers in China who may or may not work under unfair labor conditions. Greek farmers, on the other hand, do tough labor under a hot sun and fresh air. Manual labor is not appreciated in our post-modern era.

It is not just the farmer's working conditions that make the exportation of foodstuff an under-appreciated economic activity, but also the benefits to the country that come from farms that are well-tended and managed.

One of the main reasons for the devastating fires of August 2007 in Greece, when over 80 humans and 70,000 animals perished, was that farms were left untended, grass overtook fields so that a small fire, flamed by ferocious winds, turned 2.3% of the land into ashes. Working farms are natural protection against the deadly fires that sweep the country every year.

Greece is not a factory for building high-tech gadgets—that would require expensive government and private investments. So it must utilize its current assets to rebuild itself. An importing nation can become more export savvy. And reap the benefits in the process.

State of Greek Health

Ioannina, April 2

What is the general health of the Greek people during this economic crisis?

The statistics are not encouraging. According to the Greek Ministry of Health (reported in *The Guardian*), there were 40% more suicides in 2011 than the previous year. While the suicide rate is still one of the lowest in Europe, it had the highest jump of any other E.U. nation. The Greek Orthodox Church refuses to bury people who commit suicide.

Distressed calls to suicide-prevention lines are ten times higher than before the economic crisis. There are now 20,000 homeless folks in downtown Athens, in a city that once prided itself for its lack of homelessness.

Most distressed by the lack of economic opportunity are women aged between thirty and fifty, and men between forty and forty-five, or prime economic earning years. The lack of meaningful work in a land with an over 21% official unemployment rate is not encouraging.

The University of Ioannina school cafeteria seems busier than I've ever seen it before; I wonder if all those lining up for the free cafeteria food are really students of the university, or simply hungry souls?

There are not too many advertisements in Greece for weight loss anymore. I suppose that is a plus. Those tacky stomach belts and creams that supposedly vanish extra flesh are gone. And *Monocle 24* reported that sexual activity in Greece has dropped by 30%, according to a recent survey.

Does all this mean that Greeks are unhealthy? Their famous Mediterranean diet, one of the healthiest in the world, has not changed. Neither has their propensity for walking. And if it's true that more urbanites are heading back to live in their villages, their health may actually improve. And Greeks are still religious, probably more than most other Europeans. This includes the young.

Religion may help the country through this difficult, difficult period. One image clings to mind. I walked to the school cafeteria to eat. It was Sunday afternoon. The cafeteria was busier than I've remembered it being on such a day. I sat down, and a few minutes later, a young man of about twenty-two sat not far in front of me, sporting a Mohawk, in ragged clothing, and with the kind of savage expression that told me he'd seen a dark side of life. His food tray was piled with more bread slices than I've ever seen a human being carry. Perhaps he had not eaten in days. I seriously doubted he was a student: he looked around as if waiting to be busted.

With measured calmness, as if springing from an ethereal source, he promptly crossed himself in big, wide, bold movements—the kind only seen in churches. By priests. And with relish, he then began eating. I could not help but grin. The state of Greek health? Things may be bad, but people still remember the basics.

2021: New 'Revolution' for Greece

Ioannina, April 2

In 1821, Greeks revolted against their Ottoman overlords, setting forth an independent movement that finally became real in 1830 with the founding of Modern Greece. It was an epic, if bloody time in the nation's history, and one that is today celebrated every March 25th as Independence Day.

The 200th anniversary of this event will arrive in nine years. During an after-dinner dessert, a colleague associated with the University of Ioannina mentioned the idea: Why not have a new "revolution" in 2021 for Greece?

He went on to explain, "Greece is in a terrible crisis and what people here need most is some vision, some goal they can work toward. And 2021 is the perfect opportunity!"

The words hit me like an earthquake. Brilliant, I thought. Greeks thirst for a vision that will lift them through the current gloom. My friend went on: "But I fear that our current politicians don't have the vision to make such a dream possible." He shook his head plaintively. "So," I began, hoping to get him out of his gloom, "would it be possible to get new faces into the Greek political scene?"

He seemed intrigued by the idea, although it was one he had probably already reflected upon. "I am not sure," he intoned.

The idea has not stopped swirling in my head since. Running throughout modern society is a concern that social institutions are no longer meeting the needs of individuals. We have a new society that is built on the foundations of the old, and there is a huge disconnect.

Our U.S. Constitution, for example, was written in the 1780s at a time when the largest companies were basically small entrepreneurial workshops with little sway in national politics. Today, they—the huge corporations—are a dominant force of society. Yet our Constitution hardly reflects this reality.

New Greek politicians would have to shake off the old clientelist system that favors connections over merit. They would have to stop answering to their benefactors and start answering to the people that actually elect them. They would have to serve a nobler purpose than receiving free tickets to the opera and a free car and driver. They must work hard and earn their living just like the rest of us.

Meaning of a Death

Ioannina, April 4

The elderly man arrived in Syntagma Square on the morning of Wednesday, April 4, 2012. All around him, hordes poured out of the metro to head to work, to go shopping, to do errands. Pigeons hovered around the main water fountain, as they always do. Folks sat on benches around the small park, as they always do. The gent hawking his bread sticks, as he has for years, was there. So was the "Lahio" (Lottery) guy. A typical Syntagma day.

The elderly man found a tree in a grassy part of the park and stopped there. Then, at some point, he raised his pistol to his head and pulled the trigger. It was shortly before 9AM. Few, if any, knew what had happened. It's a noisy place. Then ugly reality hit. Police came. And his body was taken away.

He was seventy-seven. A handwritten note in red ink was later found, claiming he had financial woes and that he did not want to be a burden to his family. He did not want to dig through garbage to forage for food. He also railed against what he called the "Tsolakoglou occupation government," referring to the administration that, under former army officer Georgios Tsolakoglou, ran Greece under the Nazis during World War II.

That was a life that ended. There are births and deaths. Raising a child. Watching football on TV. The day in and day out of life. Now all gone. All history.

The tragedy is all too real. Too painful. Too awful to contemplate. Such events become more magnified during economic downturns, as Greece now suffers through.

Later on the same day, some 2,000 gathered in Syntagma to protest peacefully over the man's suicide. The story has been widely reported in the nation's press. Statements came from as far as the Prime Minister, Lucas Papademos. A nation has been shaken and moved. It's a harsh time in Greece, the worst in decades. Life can be cruel. Few of us can escape its bounds, its limitations, its demands. We know at the end of the day money makes our lives; it makes us who we are. Without it, we become less than humans. Or so it seems. We may not see other choices.

It's a sad day.

Internet and the Land: A Love Story?

Ioannina, April 5

It's raining in Ioannina today. Sweet, gentle, kind rain. The kind that falls after a harsh heat wave. We are forced to stay indoors and think.

A philosopher (I think it was Kant) once said that all our problems start when we leave our house. If we all stayed home more, we'd have fewer problems. At least 80% of the people own their own homes in Greece, one of the highest home ownership rates in the world. They can stay home and wait out the rain or any other inclement weather. And wait it out they must. Out in the villages and the hinterlands of Greece, the economic situation is less acute because the rhythm of life is slower. In Athens, built on its commercial operations and consumption, the economy can play havoc—great when it's good, awful when it tanks. Here in Ioannina, people live by the land and by a slower economy. There were never that many commercial shops to begin with here in Ioannina. Yes, there are some closures; this is to be expected, but nothing like the devastation in central Athens. As the economy continues to shrink (by 5% expected for this year), the backbone of this country continues to hold it together. Gandhi once said that India is made up of 700,000 villages, not the big cities but her little hamlets. Greece is made up of 6,000 villages, many of them old-folks homes devoid of life. There's a joke in my own village in Euboea: the cemetery population rises as the village population shrinks.

That may be changing. Folks are moving back to villages. Life once more returns to the hinterland. The impact of this phenomenon cannot be understated. It is a paradigm shift of large proportion, going against the grain of modern civilization.

Meanwhile, I can imagine what the return to villages means to the soul of this country. It's getting back to basics. Going back to the simple. The slow. The mundane. The rustic. But how long will it last? Can we expect young people, so used to culture and stimulation, to give up the city life? Can the Internet give what the city once gave us? Not small questions, these, but deserving of thoughtful contemplation.

Greek Survival—The 'Yiayia' Spirit!

Ioannina, April 5

Every nation faces hardship, but out of it usually comes a change, a different course, a better future. Why? Because pain forces us to reflect, to face our demons, and to let go of the past. And so it is with Greece.

Will the economy in Greece improve soon? Even the experts

don't seem to agree. Some even forecast another bailout package — the third of its kind. Schools may be shut. More layoffs are in the offing. Tourism, strained by bad images of Greece in the globe's media networks, is not the panacea it once was. What is this country to do?

I offer no solutions, but I want to speak a moment about the Greek spirit — and it begins with my grandmother. She was twenty-seven years old with three children and a four-month old baby when her husband was killed by Greek resistance in 1943 for being a collaborator—which he wasn't. Suddenly, because of this terrible mistake, she was a widow with four mouths to feed and no husband. And no food; it was war, after all. What was she to do?

The area around Euboea where she lived (where I was born) has deposits of coal. However, coal mining was under government control. To sell it openly was illegal. You could mine coal for our own needs but not sell it commercially.

My grandmother took a risk in loading up a donkey at night, under cover of darkness, and going around the local villages to sell coal for home heating. It was very dangerous, for at any time someone could report her to the authorities, and she would find herself in prison. Who would raise her children then?

How did she manage to sell coal at night and still nurse her baby? How did she survive the terrible war against the Nazis and the equally if not more devastating Civil War that followed and see her four children grown?

I knew her as someone who I hated as a child. She was fierce. She had a hearty laugh, but she also had a ferocious will, a mind-bending temper, and you did not cross her. She adored my older brother but disliked me. My brother was the more rugged, outdoor type, who helped tend her flock of goats as we were growing up. I was the stuffy intellectual, more comfortable in a school environment surrounded by books. I was forced to sleep in the same bed as her because we didn't have enough beds. She called me a "donkey" because I turned often in my sleep, and I would sometimes accidentally kick her.

It would take decades before we began to respect each other. She had an honesty that cut through the crap, the bull of life. And it stung sometimes. It took a while to get used to, but once I did, I realized what a gem she was. I was very sad when she passed away.

What made her survive through her early tragedies? It's a spirit visible in the people today. You simply must take tragedy and find a way out of it. There is no choice. There is no commercial break. There is no lifeline. There is no emergency phone call to the therapist at night. There are no special pills. It's called survival.

Whatever fate befalls Greece matters little; her people will get through it. This is a nation of some of the toughest hombres and senoritas on the globe. They will eat their young before they will surrender or give up — and it is this spirit that is now called upon to get this proud nation through a very harsh period.

Death of a Pensioner

Ioannina, April 6

He was a fruit vendor in Tunisia who daily navigated the shoals and demands of corruption to keep his little street cart business alive. It was a tough living—dealing with price swings, venal police officers constantly hassling him, fickle customers who expected the best fruit at the cheapest prices. Never a dull moment, never a "normal" day.

Government officials were the worst: their surly attitudes toward anyone they didn't like (not part of their circle of family and friends) made life hell. December 17, 2010 was another typical day. The vendor started selling at 8 A.M., but by 10:30 the cops came to hassle him. There are conflicting reports whether street vending is legal in Tunisia or not.

Then a forty-five year-old female municipal officer came by his stand and snatched his scales. He pleaded with her to return them but she refused.

The vendor bought a can of gasoline from a nearby gas station, poured it on himself, and set himself on fire. It was 11:30 A.M. Two weeks later, on January 4, 2011, Mohamed Bouazizi died from severe burn wounds to his body. The shock of his death set off protests in Tunisia that eventually toppled its government—and later those of Egypt and Libya. We now call it the Arab Spring.

When Dimitris Christoulas shot himself last Wednesday morning in Syntagma Square, few could have predicted that his suicide would set off a huge internal debate in Greece about the current economic crisis and how the political class in the country is handling it. Since his death, there have been nightly protests in Syntagma. Does this herald a new "Arab Spring" in Greece? It's too early to tell, but something is happening around Christoulas's suicide. One feels the rumblings of a powerful and upwelling force at this unfortunate death. People in Greece cannot stop talking about it. There have been some minor scuffles with the police, but the protests in Syntagma have otherwise been civil and dignified.

Rebuilding a Nation: The Social Contract

Ioannina, April 8

When modern democracy began with the American Revolution in 1776, the social contract assumed that the citizens and the state had an equal exchange: citizens gave up some of their rights in return for the state's protection, while citizens could speak and write freely and the state respected the general will of the people.

The political class that arose from modern democracy was challenged to maintain these ties to the people. But it was, and is, difficult. Why? As any leader will ask you: when does one lead the people and when does one follow them? In the first instance, a leader knows best and asks the people to follow. An example is Abraham Lincoln freeing the slaves when so much of the nation was against it. In the second, leaders follow the people's will—as happened in 1974 when the U.S. got out of the unpopular war in Vietnam.

In Greece, there has never really been a social contract between the citizens and the state. When the modern Greek state formed in 1830, after a bloody liberation movement against the Ottoman Turks beginning in 1821, a messy republic was born that soon became a monarchy without a compass or a rudder. Although largely the creation of the Great Western Powers (Great Britain, France, and Russia), Greece was an orphan child from the start—no natural mother or father in its own political aspiration.

Greece became the plaything of the Great Western Powers; they dictated how Greece as a brand would be sold to the world and how it would become a museum nation to feed the classics-starved Europeans in their quest for high culture and sophisticated aesthetics. And no civilization ever reached higher states of art and aesthetics than the ancient Greeks, so there was a lot to draw from. But modern Greece was not a real nation, but a playpen for the rich and elite. Eventually, that stretched to regular tourists who now make up its largest income-producing industry.

Without a proper social contact, first it was forced to deal with the language issue—should Greeks speak their common demotic tongue, like most countries do, or take on the patois of a new, dignified "katharevousa" version that was an update of the classical Greek variety? While other nations busily industrialized themselves, and therefore built up their economies, incredibly enough Greece fought an internal war over what language to speak.

Then there was the conflict with Turkey, going on for decades, which in 1922 finally resulted in the disaster in Smyrna that reduced the Greek population in Asia Minor to a mere trickle and left Greece wounded for decades to come. So much for its "Big Idea" of reuniting all Greek populations under one large national umbrella.

And now the economic crisis. So Greece is still not a fully-developed nation. It has been a nation in name, but its people have never really participated in its running or determined its future. It still stumbles from chaos to chaos, without discernible end. Promises are made and broken, dreams built up and taken away, goals tantalizingly close but, in the end, they too vanish. How long before the people of Greece demand a social contract?

Rebuilding a Nation: Social Contract, Pt. 2

Ioannina, April 9

Trees have cultural significance in Greece. The tree in the Garden of Eden is only one symbol; there is the olive tree in ancient Greek society. Jesus was betrayed next to a tree. And so forth.

Last Saturday, a group of mourners from the suicide of the seventy-seven year-old pensioner were in Syntagma Square after the funeral at Athens Cemetery. Two police officers happened to emerge from the metro station there when suddenly the crowd attacked them, removing the jacket and gun case from one of them. They also took his bullet-proof vest and belt. In the scuffle, the officer suffered head injuries that required hospitalization. Then the mob took the jacket and gun case and placed them on the tree where the pensioner had killed himself.

The crowd was angry and took it out on the two cops. No doubt it was an infantile way to act, to lash out at innocent people in hope of releasing anger. But it only contributes to more hysteria and anger. One feels part of the society ripping at the seams. The fabric of life has markedly changed in the past four years, and nothing seems to be healing it. The nation verges on the precipice of self-inflicted insanity that will only inflame and worsen an already insane situation.

No one can view what happened to the two officers with anything but disgust and pain. It is easy to condemn the cops as being part of a corrupt state, but if this is the best that we as a society can do (and here I place myself in the camp of Greeks), things are not looking too good.

This week, the Seamen's Union will go on strike, shutting down ferry service for the country. This comes at a crucial time for Easter travelers and only hurts a weakened tourist industry. Farmers and tourist officials begged the Union to drop the strike, but they voted to go ahead—even if this meant catastrophe for other groups in Greece. And such is life here—one group makes demands that satisfy themselves but hurts others, and nothing stops them from making such demands. In the end, all groups are hurt because all groups suffer from the demands made. We are all branches of the same tree.

Rebuilding a Nation: Branding Greece!

Ioannina, April 10

In a speech on 6 December 2011, advertising manager Peter Economides gave a rousing speech about "re-branding" Greece. He was one of the folks responsible for re-branding Apple in 1997 when it was a near bankrupt corporation. Hardly anyone could imagine then what Apple is today—the world's biggest corporation by shareholder value.

In the speech, Economides discusses the value of branding. First, he tells us, "brand" refers to what people think of you. "Branding" is the process by which you manage your brand. Two different animals, apparently. Greece has got an image problem. People associate it with corruption, laziness, debt, and incompetence. Is this the whole picture? And how do we change the image?

Further, he claims, we must get all 10.8 million Greeks aboard the branding vision. It's another version of democracy, but this one involves how we can collectively come up with a vision of how others in the world can regard us. We may laugh at this scenario, except that we do so at our own peril. For the fact is, ours is an image-industry civilization. We eat, breath, swallow, and think in images. Our lives have become one string of images. Film historian Neal Gabler calls it "lifie" (comparing it to movies).

We have internalized images so much that we have turned our lives into walking movies. We are our own movies—directed, written, and starring ourselves. And we try to take on any role we wish. It's an extraordinary time in human history. It's also a fact of modernity.

Economides touches upon this reality—that images make us who we are. We are the sum total of our images, our presentation to the world. And right now Greece suffers from a terrible image problem. The way we Greeks get into the news is by our pensioners committing suicide (how often does that happen in the developed world and get reported the same way?) or when angry citizens throw yogurt at our politicians.

But are we talking about creating a "Potemkin village?"—an image of Greece that hides the ugly truth merely for the sake of attracting tourists? Economides wants us to look into the Greek DNA and come up with a vision of what a better Greece looks like. He tells us that branding is about community—that it can only work if the population is behind the image. It must be an authentic image. It must resonate with Greece and Greeks and with the rest of the globe. It must be based on something truly Greek.

But what is this image?

Grim News: Greek Unemployment Rising

Ioannina, April 12

It now stands at 21.8%. A record for Greece and more than double the seventeen-country Eurozone average. In real figures, this means 1,084,668 people are unemployed out of a total Greek population of 10.8 million. Astonishing. And it will not get better any time soon.

On one level, these are merely numbers, but numbers always mask the individuals behind them. Those people are faceless. Just statistics. Economists tell us that the high unemployment is necessary to reduce labor costs that were (until recently) 20% higher than Germany's workforce, incredible as that sounds. The high unemployment rate is sending down labor costs that eventually helps the economy, and brings in much-needed investment. But tell that to the person who has no job and must feed his or her family.

At times, it feels that human beings are caught up in a spider's web. Loss of a job not only devastates a family's finances, but it makes the future seem very, very bleak. We hear that Greece might return to growth in 2013, but it was also forecast in 2010 by the Greek Finance Ministry that growth would return in 2012. Has it? Will it?

A climate of fear and worry in Greece makes the future seem too distant and far away to consider. It is splashed across the people's faces—the grim reality that life is not what it used to be. A proud nation is faced with a dilemma: how to move forward? What to do? What to think? Say? Feel? In an earlier entry, I talked about my grandmother and the tragedies of her life—losing her husband at twenty-seven in 1943, raising three children and a new baby, selling coal illegally in the middle of the night to bring food to their mouths—these are not just stories, but they have now become mythic in my family.

When the times were good in Greece in the early 2000s, such memories seemed quaint and silly. Consumption was rising in Greece, cheap money was everywhere, and prices and goods just kept rising and rising. It was a selfish time. That era is gone. I remember once a World War II veteran telling me that Greece was a devastated place in the 1940s, yet despite the horrors, he's never seen people as generous and unselfish as during that time. He lamented that it was gone forever.

He may be wrong. The recent suicide of the seventy-seven year-old pensioner and the reaction it got from Greek residents says unselfishness may be coming back. If so, it comes back during a critical period. And it may be a way out of this sad time.

Rebranding a Nation: The Environment

Ioannina, April 13

Outside my window of the guesthouse here at the University of Ioannina in Northern Greece is a view of a lusciously green hillside. To the right are spectacular mountains, which in the past few days have gotten a brand new coat of snow.

To say that this environment is rich is too obvious. I am not a bird expert, but the variety of birds in this area is astonishing. My walks to the cafeteria are serenaded by the most mellifluous bird sounds I have ever heard. Yet, how many people around the world know about the rich environmental heritage of Greece? Such a small country, such a vast variety of environments. Desert. Alpine terrain. Swamps. Lakes. Mountains. A veritable treasure chest of beauty, yet most of us only know the beaches and Zorba the Greek.

I cannot think of a better rebranding of Greece than to showcase her extraordinary environment. The problem is that Greeks have been bad stewards of this precious geography. This poetic landscape is littered with empty plastic water bottles and felled trees. Since illegal home building is almost encouraged by the state, which lacks the capacity to enforce the rules, the environment continues to lose ground to development. And now, at a time of deep economic malaise, which is more important, the environment or the people?

For this rebranding to work, a new attitude must be fostered in people. It can happen. It will mean better stewardship of the environment and better protection for her forests. It will mean a real concern for how we treat our precious ecology. We should set new standards in environmental protection. It cannot be otherwise. It would involve the promotion of marine parks, for example. What Greece has in the way of her ecology is a great, great gift, almost as great (some say greater!) than the oversold classical legacy of her past. Up to this point, we have done a lousy job of protecting this legacy; in fact, we leave a ruined geography, as we have done since antiquity. Read Plato. He talks about the destruction of the environment.

Such knowledge is in the Greek DNA. But can Greece set an example for the rest of the world? If laws were actually enforced, then the rebranding of Greece on an ecological basis can happen. This will require a new kind of Greek state, but it's possible. Right now anything is possible. That's the encouraging truth about the grim Greek reality.

Rise of Greek Extremism

Ioannina, April 13

Greece has suffered through political instability since its founding in 1830, when its first leader was assassinated. Economic default is nothing new to the country (it has defaulted at least five times, perhaps more), and the land of the birth of democracy has also been the land of secret populism—for the order and stability that dictatorship brings. The economic meltdown now in progress has only exacerbated political instability. This, coupled with unpoliced borders and the influx of hundreds of thousand of immigrants looking for work, has put pressure on both the state and the population.

Enter "Golden Dawn" (Chrysi Avgi). This is an extreme right-wing group that seems to pay tribute to both Nazism and dictatorship. By dictatorship, I mean the type that ran Greece from 1967 to 1974. Many regard that period as a halcyon of stability and economic progress. Sadly, they are right. But it came at a high price. That price was the dissolution of democracy and the rise of authoritarianism.

The colonels that ran Greece during those seven years may have done some good, at least initially, but because power corrupts and absolute power corrupts absolutely, in time its regime devolved into petty squabbles and power games usually reserved for movies about the Borgias or corrupt Popes in the Middle Ages. I watched in astonishment on TV last summer during riots outside of the Parliament building in downtown Athens as a group of thugs attacked violent anarchists and afterwards escaped through the cordon of police officers. Many in Greece have long claimed that the Golden Dawn heavies are in secret alliance with the police to deal with the anarchists that destroy downtown Athens in every major demonstration. Now, with 3% of the popular vote and seemingly on the cusp of being elected to the

71

Greek Parliament for the first time, fear has spread through parts of the political landscape.

Golden Dawn exploits people's anger against the austerity measures imposed by the Europeans. For them, "banksters," as they like to call bankers, lie at the heart of the devastation of Greece. Who funds this strange brew of a political party seems to be unknown. It's not just the Nazi salutes or the Nazi-like insignia, or the menace they offer to immigrants. We've seen this type of savagery in other European countries. And truly astonishing is their rising popular support. Is this how Greece really wants to be known to the world? My family left Greece shortly after the Junta took power in 1967. I can scarcely believe my eyes that this awful period is coming back to haunt Greece. There's a video in Greek, in which we see Nikolaos Michaloliakos, Golden Dawn's leader, in action, giving the Nazi salute, with his two thugs as bodyguards, in a meeting of the Athens City Council, where he happened to win a seat as a council member in 2010.

Greece heads down a dangerous path.

Rebranding Greece: Taxi Drivers

Ioannina, April 16

Athens is like New York. You develop a thick skin to survive; otherwise, you will be run over by a semi.

If you've spent any time in Greek cabs, you will encounter *them*! The taxi drivers from hell! I refer to the drivers who charge triple the listed price, or who fail to turn on the meter and demand more than the normal amount, or who take side roads to increase the fares, or who seem to be on drugs and drive like maniacs . . . it's endless.

The thirty-five euro price from Athens International Airport to downtown Athens is the law, but apparently many taxi-drivers see it only as a suggestion. They usually target tourists who they know are usually tired and barely awake after a long trans-Atlantic trip—and won't fight back if overcharged.

I once got into a taxi cab and apparently made a grammatical mistake, which the driver immediately took offense to. He proceeded to yell at me about it, demanding that I correct myself. I told him to mind his own business, but he kept chattering. Mercifully, he didn't overcharge. I confess that I've been wimpy about refusing to pay high fares, or saying something when receiving bad service. But I've learned to fight back. I have yet to get into a shouting match with a taxi driver, but I am prepared to do that if it is necessary. If we don't stand up, then these driver-thieves will continue to exploit people. I notice that those cab drivers who start a conversation with me are more than likely to rip me off. So I keep my mouth shut or tell them politely and firmly that I am not interested in chatting. I presume that sends them a signal that I am not to be trifled with.

Can anything be done about it? We should fight back. Refuse to pay exorbitant fees. It would also help if the state could do background checks on all potential cabbies prior to giving them their licenses. Perhaps we can also start a list of rip-off cabbies and make this available to anyone who wants it. Then, when you are standing in line waiting for a taxi at the airport, you could type in the cabbie's license plate on your smart phone to see if it matches a list of rip-off taxi drivers. Cleaning up its taxi drivers from hell would be one way to rebrand Greece!

Rebuilding a Nation: Family!

Ioannina, April 17

Last Sunday was Greek Easter, the biggest holiday in the country. Everyone gathered for the obligatory family meal, this year with the solemnity of the economic crisis hanging in the air. Despite the financial woes, such events are important markers in Greek lives. We temporarily forget our pain and give thanks to this life—and to each other. We find solace and comfort in such moments, knowing that we are not alone, and despite the economic cruelty, we can still laugh, we can still eat, we can still drink, we can still enjoy each other's company. When younger, I never really liked such events. I found them boring and stultifying. They seemed like forced social obligation rather than comfort. As I grow older, I am more and more impressed by certain social rites that now seem very profound to me.

There is no economic measurement for families getting together over meals, yet its social capital is beyond monetary value. Imagine if family were not so important in Greek society—how much would the state have to spend to maintain order and equanimity in society? Families can be dysfunctional, but they also keep community together, check our egos, and remind us that we are humble flecks on this earth.

Suicide and homelessness would be greater in Greece were it not for strong family bonds. The political system here does not generally serve them well, forcing families to fight each other for meager resources. It may even take families for granted, rather than paying fealty to them.

Leaders need to recognize and appreciate how vital families are to society's well being. They should ask for their help during this hard time. Greece is made up less by individuals and more by families. They are the central unit of society. By turning to them and asking that family members support each other during this crucial period, leaders would take a big step towards providing some solace and comfort right now when it is sorely needed.

President Franklin D. Roosevelt did this brilliantly in the early 1930s during the Great Depression with his "fireside chats." He spoke to families on the radio, and they sat around the living room and listened. They got through the difficulty and became a stronger nation together. No one speaks to families in Greece like that. No one has taken the time to reach out in that fashion. There is no need to suffer this economic crisis in silence. Greece has been through worse difficulties—famine, invasion, disease, war—and still survived. This country made it through because of the family, and it can once more be the bedrock of a new emerging nation.

Fate of Nations: Crimes & Politics

Ioannina, April 18

Being in government involves intelligence, cunning, determination and political instincts. It's a unique, demanding job that fulfills certain aspirations in the holder. It's also about power.

Power does strange things to human beings. Apostolos "Akis" Tsochadzopoulos was in the 1970s a founding member of PASOK, or the liberal party of Greece. When Andreas Papandreou, the father of PASOK, won election in 1981, Akis was invited to be Minister of Public Works, having been elected to Parliament. It was a heady time for Greece. It had joined the European Union the same year and Papandreou was poised to alter the political landscape.

Papandreou developed close economic ties with the Arabic world, particularly Colonel Muammar Gaddafi of Libya, but also used the Greek civil service to give jobs to voters. It was the start of the bloated Greek state and the political parties of Greece becoming piggy banks to their voters. Papandreou did not start this corrupt system, but he certainly expanded it.

Meanwhile, Akis climbed the political ladder. He led the ministries of the Interior and Transport and Communication. Then in 1996 he became Minister of Defense, one of the top offices in the cabinet. Defense ministers purchase military hardware for the country. He seemed to favor German products. Akis had the look of shrewdness about him; his mean, cobra stare was the hallmark of a man not to be trifled with. And he had power.

In 2004, Akis had no ordinary wedding. He married in Paris with a reception at the ultra-rich Four Seasons Hotel with a view of the Eiffel Tower. Extravagant or a show of power? Then in May 30, 2010, *Kathimerini* in Greece broke the story that his wife had purchased an expensive home across from the Acropolis just a few days before Parliament passed a vote to raise real estate taxes and curb tax evasion. The mansion was purchased from an off-shore company.

As he did with other accusations, Akis threatened to take such allegations to court. It was bullying but it was also a show of his will. The scandals continued, and Akis was implicated in the Siemens scandal involving bribes paid by the German electronic firm to Greek politicians for purchase of the company's products. Then there was a scandal involving kickbacks for the purchase of expensive German submarines. All under Akis's watch.

Akis is not having a good 2012. Right now he is sitting in a jail in Piraeus along with relatives and associates. Akis's cell is the same one occupied by the former chief monk of Vatopedi Monastery. The monk had a lot of power too, and he used it to get the Greek government under New Democracy head and prime minister, Costas Karamanlis, to swap land that netted the Monastery 100 million euros.

Things don't look good for Akis. And his jailing comes at a bad time for PASOK. The party is a shell of its former self, having sunk in the polls in the past three years as a result of its handling of the country's economy. The new PASOK leader, replacing George Papandreou, son of Andreas, is Evangelos Venizelos. He has worked hard to resurrect PASOK's image, but the sight of Akis in all the media being arrested does not help his cause. Was it coincidental that Akis's arrest came during a run-up to the coming national elections on May 6, 2012? At a time when New Democracy under Antonis Samaras seeks a mandate from the Greek populace?

Power does strange things to human beings.

[Editor's note: Akis was sentenced on October 7, 2013 to twenty years in prison.]

Rebuilding a Nation: Family, Part 2!

Ioannina, April 19

We are presented with a stark contrast—our lives, our jobs, our relationships can be lived with almost mechanical determination, or we can enjoy life with mindful practice, with passion and zest.

There are two sides to the Greek ethos: the extraordinary work ethic of men and women who work more hours than most Europeans, and the other side that is often celebrated as "Zorba." Too often Greeks are known by Zorba and not enough by the tremendous labor, sweat, and grit they contribute every day.

My family knew both. I grew up amazed at the work being done around me, yet also recall with fondness the times when we celebrated in between all the hard labor. When my family moved to the United States, the first thing I experienced was the work ethic, with fewer celebrations. American culture does not always permit celebration of the kind we had known back in the old country—Easter feasts, big fat Greek weddings, baptisms, and "panagiria" (festivals).

Suddenly, the words of a man I had met on a return trip to Greece haunted me. It was in a nearby village from mine on the Greek island of Euboea that I was shocked one summer to find an American who was at one of those great panagiria that take place in the region every mid-August—the Virgin Mary's Festival. Chatting with him, I asked him what he was doing there in the middle of nowhere. "I came here to celebrate this festival. To enjoy life. That's what we don't do back home and what is done here!" He looked around at all the families gathered; nary a sad face in the lot. All for a few hours of forgetting their troubles and concerns, and enjoying the music, the dancing, the food, the company. My earliest images of village life were the families, mine as well as those around me—both relatives and neighbors. It was the core of community life, and in a strange sense, and not always easily or without argument, there was a feeling that the families bound up in the community represented the natural order of existence.

I was shocked therefore to arrive in the U.S. and be presented with a different picture—families were not the center of life, children often had to leave the home at 18, families sometimes seemed more like a mini-corporation than a living embodiment of our human needs and aspirations.

It took a while to digest this new reality. I always imagined the village life I knew in the past and became sentimental for it. I was unhappy during my first few years in America. One day, out of great despondency, I told my mother that I was going back to Greece, even if it meant getting there by foot! I think about family now, because it is a cornerstone of the human spirit. It is where we train to become human beings. Nothing can substitute for it. And yet its fragility is evident; not all countries ascribe to close-knit families. Many Western cultures positively fight against it.

The temptation is to do your own thing, live your life, be independent, be strong. I don't deny any of those rights. But they are not mutually exclusive of the acceptance of family. Family is, after all, for better or worse, the center of our most treasured moments and the place where we first learn to love.

Fate and Image: Greece's Iwo Jima

Ioannina, April 20

A newspaper photo of a group of workers hoisting a new Greek flag atop the Parliament building in downtown Athens immediately brings to mind the famous photograph of the five American marines and one Navy corpsman hoisting the U.S. flag atop Mt. Suribachi on the Pacific island of Iwo Jima in 1945. The mountain had just been captured from the Japanese after a ferocious and devastating fight. The Iwo Jima photo quickly became an iconic image, very popular with readers of newspapers and reprinted in many publications. I am not certain that the same will happen with the hoisting of the Greek flag, but I can't help being drawn to the similarities between the two images. I am sure the photographer—Yannis Behrakis of Reuters—was aware of this.

Why do some images become iconic or so easily recognizable in the culture? Do they strike at a deep chord in audiences? The photos of Iwo Jima and the Greek flag share a certain symmetry. They both have beautiful aesthetic value—the way they are beautifully framed—and there is movement in each picture that immediately captures the eye. Yet something happens that goes beyond the framing and composition of the photos. The bloody battle that led to the hoisting of the flag at Iwo Jima is implied in the picture: The loss of life, the pain and suffering that it took to raise this flag. We are moved by the circumstances, as we are by the feelings, that there was victory at the end. We appreciate, or at least become aware, of the tremendous sacrifices involved.

The raising of the Greek flag over the Parliament offers the same symbolism. The country has gone through a lot in the past three years since it needed a bailout to survive. Four years in recession. Unemployment at 21.8%. Pensions cut. Lives ruined. Businesses wrecked. Yet, the flag is raised. Greece is not dead. The economic war continues, but here at last is a small victory.

And I can't help but be flushed with emotion seeing this. This little country that seems to suffer in dramatic fashion still survives. Still fights. Still hoists its flag on top of its symbol of democracy.

It's a beautiful moment, and one that can't entirely be expressed into words. That is the power of iconic photos—they capture feelings, thoughts, hopes, fears, and desires that otherwise are left unsaid. It's strange to feel hope in a time of great suffering. I think about my own periods of sadness, and it was hard to imagine there could be light at the end of the tunnel. But the light did come, and the dark days did end. If nothing else, the raising of the Greek flag represents that bit of hope.

It is not over. The fight continues. The flag is raised!

WWII grenades found in potatoes from Germany to Greece

Ioannina, April 20

A shipment of potatoes from Germany sent to Greece contained two WWII hand grenades. The grenades were inactive. They were found at a potato processing factory in Atalanti in the Northern Attica region about two-hours north of Athens. The first grenade was discovered when workers at the factory heard strange sounds coming from the machine that washes the potatoes. Later, the second grenade was found. Police are investigating the source of the grenades.

This incident is sure to raise anti-German sentiment in a country already with a high pitch of such sentiments since the imposition of austerity measures in Greece in 2010. Many Greeks blame Germany, and in particular, Chancellor Angela Merkel, for what they feel to be oppressive measures against them. Unemployment is nearly 22% in Greece, and salaries and pensions have been greatly reduced as a result of the austerity measures.

Yet many economists insist that these measures are necessary to bring Greece's economy in line with European standards. In recent months there have been demonstrations in front of the German Embassy in Athens, with Greek protesters dressed as Nazi officers. German residents in Athens have also felt the hostility. German tourists bookings are down as a result, further hurting the economy of Greece, as Germans make up one of the largest groups of visitors to the Mediterranean nation.

Mist & Snow: Weather in Ioannina

Ioannina, April 21

The words of W.B. Yeats come to mind:
> *Bolt and bar the shutter*
> *For the foul winds blow*
> *Our minds are at their best this night*
> *And I seem to know*
> *That everything outside us is*
> *Mad as the mist and snow.*

When I arrived in Ioannina at the end of March, the weather was pleasant. Then about midway through April, it turned wet and cold. The surrounding mountains, whose snow was melting as we started our study abroad program here, are now packed with the white stuff. And in the past few days, there's been more rain, more cold. And thunder. It cracked like a herd of stampeding buffaloes yesterday! In a poll in the U.S., the public regarded recent weather changes as a manifestation of global warming. Most scientists are sure the recent weather phenomena is a sign of climate change. The public poll may not accurately reflect a belief in the certainty of global warming itself, but a civilization informed by images. The scientific revolution that began in the

15th century in Europe, with the aid of Arabs, brought to the fore the power of empirical evidence (or the results of experiments being visible, not hidden or unknown). Coupled with the explosion of printing after 1453, science took on new majesty that it never had before.

This did not eliminate superstition; that remains with us. But it did marginalize it as primitive and unscientific. Superstition is where the stereotype of the pre-industrial native, the men in loincloths in the jungle, as being inferior, took on currency. You get a whiff of that by reading Jonathan Swift's *Gulliver's Travels* or Daniel Defoe's *Robinson Crusoe*.

Science was always predicated on the written word, hence the importance of publishing scientific studies so that others could replicate them and prove them right. But in the 1950s a remarkable change began to take place. Television. Suddenly, the primacy of the written word lost steam. The visual rose in ascendancy. We read less and watched more. Newspaper readership eventually took a nosedive.

As words lost their power and hold on civilization, superstition and the mystical crept back into society. Logic, so much at the center of a print-oriented society, lost sway to magic and the supernatural. Ghost stories seem real to us now. And very popular. The planet has gone through many climatic changes. It's been warmer and colder than what we have now. Are we headed for a catastrophic climate change due to human-made pollution? We have affected the planet. No one on this earth can be proud of our environmental record. There seems hardly a river left on the planet from which you can dip and drink a handful of water.

Every time there's strange weather, is it because of global warming? Scientists don't know, and this is worrisome. Perhaps this worry has a silver lining. Perhaps it will get us to think about how we treat the environment. Mother Earth is a tough cookie, but there are limits. It is the focus on the superstitious that raises red flags. It is an anxious civilization we live in.

Miracle On Thin Ice? Greek Hockey Skates On!

Ioannina, April 22

They wear pads, skates, gloves, and use sticks just like hockey players in Canada, Russia, Sweden or the U.S. The difference? They're Greek! Shades of Jamaica's sledding team?

Hockey began in Greece in 1984 with returning natives who brought the game from abroad. Five league teams formed that year, and the first game was played in Athens in 1985. But not in a regulation skating rink. That came four years later. In 1992 came the first miracle. The first Greek National Hockey Team was formed from the league players, and with only two weeks of practice, it flew to South Africa for the World Hockey Championships, Division III. With Greeks from South Africa cheering them on, they won bronze medals!

Triumph, then heartache. A small grant from the Greek Undersecretary of State for Sport that had helped them along stopped in 1993. It was a rollercoaster ride from the beginning, but without funding, players drifted away or quit playing. It was a struggle even finding a proper sized skating rink, never mind that few Greeks watched the games or fewer still followed the national team. It seemed impossible for the team to hang on. Every practice, every game took on special significance.

The Greek National Hockey Team continued to participate in World Championships, but by 2002, the league teams had disappeared. In 2003, for further humiliation, the last ice rink in Greece shut down. More players quit. It truly seemed the end. But somehow, the spirit would not die. Players and coaches remained, and they decided to continue practicing—in the Czech

Republic—with players and coaches paying their own way there and back. Plans were made for the World Championships to take place in Greece in 2010.

The hope was that this would put ice hockey on the map in Greece. Hard work and hopes dug hard for this dream. But the games were cancelled for financial reasons and had to be moved to Luxembourg.

Despite the devastating news, the Greeks rallied and, incredibly, won a silver medal there! This victory gave the team hope that ice hockey would continue in Greece. The financial situation worsened, but the players refused to give up. The World Championships were held in Turkey this month. The opening game was between Greece and Turkey, with the Turkish team crushing their neighbors, 6-1. Rather than being devastated, the Greeks were happy with how they played.

Cross-cultural ethnic tensions that had marred previous matches were not there this time. The two teams fought on the ice, not off the rink. Sport triumphed over politics, for the moment at least. It was a tough tournament for the Greeks. They lost four games in a row. But in their last game against Mongolia last Friday, they came out on top, 4-1.

It's easy to get jaded in sports. Big money, corruption, big egos. But here's one sport where it's just the game and the thrill of playing it. In the sports-entertainment complex, this is a miracle.

Fate of Nations: Ioannina's Jews

Ioannina, April 23

The synagogue is located just inside the old castle by the lake in Ioannina. I walked inside the ramparts, swung left, and after about twenty meters arrived at the neo-classical entrance on the right.

The caretaker of the synagogue told me the building dates

from 1829. The exterior of the structure shows its age, but the inside is bathed in soft, pastel-like light. Under this gentle glow, the interior walls revealed plaques with the names of 1,850 Jews taken by Nazis in 1944 who later died in the concentration camps. Children. Aunts. Uncles. Fathers. Mothers. Grandpas. Grandmas. Sisters. Brothers. Friends. All here. All dead. All mourned. Black and white photos below the names reveal some of their faces.

An older couple entered the building. Age gives dignity to humans, and they both carried it with particular grace and solemnity. The woman, Stella Koen, 85, asked me where I was from. I told her, and then I asked about her time in Ioannina. She rolled up her sleeve and showed us the concentration camp number on her arm. She recalled being led away to Auschwitz. "And we survived," she whispered glumly. Her pale eyes clouded with fear and revulsion when she talked about the neo-Nazis of today's Greece, the Golden Dawn party, and the dangers they pose to Greek society. The day before, 100 members of Golden Dawn showed up at a political rally for a PASOK (liberal) member of Parliament; they taunted him and threw coffee cups and water bottles at him!

An American couple in their 60s, Diana Dostis and her husband Isaak Dostis, transplants from New York, stepped inside the synagogue, and I was introduced to them. The couple both spoke enthusiastically about their work preserving the Jewish culture in Ioannina. Isaak beamed with pride about his video projects and about the mayor of Ioannina, who lied to the Nazis during the occupation in the 1940s and claimed the building was a library, not a synagogue, and therefore saved it from destruction.

Then the service started. We sat down and fell silent. The dignified old man, Samuel Koen, sat at a table in the middle of the sanctuary and read from the Torah. It was cold in the room, but his words strangely warmed me inside. It was a short service, about half an hour. He asked if anyone wanted to speak. There were no more than thirty individuals in the congregation, seated by gender. One serious-looking man, Moise Elisaf, stood up to speak.

"The egg of the serpent is incubating again," the man warned grimly, referring to Golden Dawn. "And there are only two things we can do. One, remember the past. And two, do all in our power to fight this scourge. I am afraid things are going to get worse, but we must draw courage from this battle!" The speech lasted about three minutes. Sweets were passed around, and we headed for a short service at a memorial just outside the castle walls.

The memorial stood next to a tourist shop. I had passed it many times in my three trips to Ioannina but never stopped to study it. How blind we are to history. The man who led the service came and again read from the Torah. We listened, the sun beaming down on us as if approving of the event. And then it was over.

The woman who survived Auschwitz started to leave. I ran after her to say good-bye. Someone called out to her, and she turned. Our eyes met and locked briefly, and she smiled at me ever so gently. I grinned back. Whatever our religion or beliefs, at that moment, we were all Jews. Then she turned, and, slowly and movingly, walked away, carried on one arm by a friend. As she left, the question came: What would the rest of us now do to face the darkening neo-fascist clouds of Europe?

Rebuilding a City: New Athens!

Ioannina, April 24

The riot images going out to the world were devastating. Not once, not twice, but several times in the past few years the world has witnessed mayhem and utter chaos ("haos," as in "house," in Greek!) taking place in downtown Athens.

Horrible to watch the destruction: Balaklava-hooded youths, breaking up the marble tiles of Syntagma Square next to the Parliament buildings and throwing the pieces at the riot police. A ki-osk ("periptero") in Syntagma set on fire, the owner losing every-thing (he did not have insurance). The square now is a pale imitation of its former glory.

Then there are the empty buildings in the Plaka in central Athens. The rash of pickpockets that now hover at Monasteraki. The constant harassment of peddlers hawking pirated music, fake Gucci handbags, and pointless trinkets. The endless tide of graf-fiti that ruins beautiful neo-classical buildings. It may be art to some, but it's visual cancer to many.

To see the majesty of this great city ruined leaves a pit in the stomach. It is like viewing a classic painting that's been torn to shreds. Downtown Athens' rents have fallen. Empty storefronts hit the eye. It seems every block in the area now has shuttered businesses. Yet out of this maelstrom rises hope. There are vi-sionaries in Greece who see a better future. These are women and men who use their entrepreneurial skills to make a better Athens today. This includes The Breeder art gallery that is also a restaurant that invites chefs to come and cook for a couple of months. Food as art, in other words.

There is the boutique in The New Hotel that offers elegance and sophistication without the pomp and circumstance of their higher priced brethren. There is the Kunsthalle art gallery in the middle of a block known for prostitution and drug-dealing, which is taking cultural chances. There is also coLab located a couple blocks from Syntagma. The premise of the company is to be an incubator for new entrepreneurs by offering a host of services (office space, meeting space, technical know-how, etc.). It is pres-ently home to sixteen start-up companies, including Historious that allows smartphone-using tourists in Athens to get steeped in the history of the area.

Many Athenians did not take the riots sitting down. Fotis I. Antonopoulos looks like an over-aged hippie with his ponytail, but he's a well-paid Web program designer who started his own olive oil marketing company, OliveShop.com. Fotis talks about the difficulty of getting a license to export from Greece, including having to give samples of his and his partners' stool to health department officials prior to approval. He didn't want to pay the so-called "speed tax" (bribery) to quicken the approval process. But now Fotis is in business and he apparently is doing well.

There is a new cultural center in the heart of Athens called Camp. They just launched a new playwriting contest involving using Page 31 of any play as source material for a new production. According to curator George Zaboulakiss on his website, Page 31 "aims toward collaboration and the exchange of ideas, promotes the research of novel aesthetic forms and alternative modes of production and relies heavily on interaction and communication with the public." I have not been able to find the significance behind why page 31, but the point is there: Athens rises.

Work of Nations: Return to Basics

Ioannina, April 25

The news brings warnings of another deep contraction of the Greek economy this year—to the tune of 5%. The country is in its fifth year of recession and has shed 17% of its economic output in that time. Tourist numbers are down so far this year, along with hotel occupancy rates, car rentals, shopping, and just about all other economic measures in Greece. There was the suicide of the seventy-seven year-old pensioner. "Suicide by economic crisis" is apparently a phrase now common with some European newspapers. And banks may be heading for nationalization. Since 2009, Greek banks have seen 70 billion euros withdrawn from their accounts, devastating their ability to lend and provide liquidity to businesses and consumers. The International Monetary

Fund, in a recent report, suggested that a return of the drachma in Greece would in the long run further destabilize the country's economy. Only by continuing to shrink its deficits and spending can Greece hope to return to economic growth. What does this mean on the ground?

Greeks seem to adjust by reducing the frivolous. Where once no one seemed to care about the plethora of plastic bottles being thrown away, now at our nearby "kilikio" (cafeteria), the operator collects all the plastic bottles and aluminum cans, which are then picked up by recyclers. In a land where recycling is only a recent phenomenon, this is a huge step. Public transportation remains vital and common. At whatever age or economic level, using the metro in Athens or the buses in Ioannina is common and cheap.

The emphasis on expensive clothing is taking a hit. Greeks tie with Italians for being the most fashion conscious (spending more on average than all other European nations on clothing!), but you see a lot of college women today in Greece wearing sneakers or canvas shoes. Entrepreneurs use the economic crisis as a jolt to unleash their ideas and innovations; this is evident in a number of new export-driven companies. Many of these folks are well-educated, global-minded types, often well-versed in English, and not willing to put up with the corruption of Greece. They want a fresh start, and they deserve it.

In many ways, the excessive consumption of the past ten years is dying and being replaced by the work ethic that I remember growing up with in Greece. Everyone worked then. Nothing was too undignified if it involved work and payment. Simple and straightforward. Modernity came with Greek membership in the European Union in 1981, and with it, the idea that work and play could go together. Fashion and gossip magazines, once quaint relics of the romantic era of the 19th century, often substituted for religion and philosophy in the 1980s.

Play could even turn into work: fashion, celebrity, style, glamour, media attention, social status—all these promised riches. This particular rocket shot up in the 1990s and reached a crescendo in the go-go years of the 2000s. Work by that point had become a four-letter word. There were millions (even billions!) to be made in the dot-com world. Work could be done in front of a laptop and bring in more money than traditional back-breaking labor.

Money freely circulated in Greece, thanks to European bankers who flooded the country with cheap loans. And how was the money spent? There is the story of the Minister of Culture (under Prime Minister Kostas Karamanlis) who gave half a million euros to the female singer who won Eurovision for Greece in 2005 (she was actually born and raised in Sweden)—just for the heck of it. He claimed that it was a way to promote Greece through her concerts, but she was doing her concerts irrespective of his donation.

When the party ended for the rich in late 2009, the extent of the excesses hung like a thick, murky cloud over the country. Little of the cheap credit went to productive output (to help build real jobs and real things in Greece), so when the economic tsunami hit, the credit bubble burst loud and strong and pathetically.

Many warned, even prior to the Athens 2004 Olympic Games, that the economy was headed for a big fall. Few listened. The party music drowned out the canary calls. Now it's 2012. Jobs are scarce, business has collapsed, there is threat of bank nationalization, and some companies are putting "drachma clauses" into their contracts with Greek businesses.

Good old-fashioned work seems like paradise now.

Fate of Nations—New Greek Diaspora

Ioannina, April 26

The exodus probably began as early as 2008, a year before Greece went into bankruptcy. In 2011, it was estimated that 70,000 Greeks emigrated to Germany alone. This is higher than folks fleeing other debt-stricken countries—Spain, Italy, and Portugal. The economic conditions are most severe in Greece compared to the other SIP nations, despite the fact that unemployment in Spain stands at 25%. Since the cost of living in Greece is higher, survival requires more income.

Greek banks face complete dissolution, since they have lost 70 billion euros of deposits in the past few years. Greeks vote with their feet; they sense difficulty and flee for the four corners of the earth. It is a nation of migrants—which is as true now as it was in classical times when cities like Athens, Chalkida, and Corinth sent their excess populations to found new colonies around the Mediterranean and the Black Sea.

The result was an explosion of trade, since those in exile demanded the products of home. Today, there is no similar trading. In this new diaspora, families and individuals flee with few tethers from home. They are completely on their own. I know the feeling. My family arrived in Seattle on a Saturday, and by Monday my brother and I were in school. We came knowing only one English word ("No") and had no preparation save for the occasional old man in our Greek village who reminded us that there would be gold in the streets of America.

It was a rapturous moment, leaving one nation for another, swapping Greece for America. Nights seemed long, days were cold. My body could not digest the new food. I had no friends in school. Worse, I had no voice. Whatever thoughts were in my head went as far as my teeth and halted there. I could not speak the language. No animal has that handicap. It took two years for me to be able to converse with others. Two years of suppressed words. Two years of suppressed thoughts. Two years of complete silence to the outside world. Only at home did I have a voice.

Now it is a blessing that my family went to America. Success has come, haltingly, but it has come. We have much to be thankful for. But none of this can remove the pain of those first few years when I became a ghost in my own body, when the outside world was a place of sheer terror and humiliation, when dignity (that peculiar aspect of the human species) was something left behind in the sun-warmed air at the airport in Athens.

Once gone from a country, you can never go back. Even when you go back, you never go back. It is similar to crossing the same river—it can never be done twice. There are thousands of such stories like mine taking place right now in Germany, Italy, England, France, the U.S., Canada, Australia, South Africa, South America. Wherever there are jobs, there are transplanted Greeks trying to adjust to the new society. If you see such a person, smile gently at them and nod. Someday sociologists will be writing about this new Greek diaspora, even sing its cultural praises.

Meanwhile, these folks just want to make life whole again.

Strays of Greece—Woe, Triumph!

Ioannina, April 27

Greeks have a complex relationship with their animals. I grew up in a house that had a horse, two goats, and several chickens.

We also had a black Labrador retriever that helped tend the goats and sheep of a great uncle who was a sheepherder. It was an extremely smart dog, but like many pets in Greece, he was never let inside the house and had to fend for himself for food. One day, a neighbor shot him dead.

I don't know if this was in the back of my mind one early September afternoon in the Plaka not long ago when I walked out of the office where I worked and suddenly saw a little kitten staggering on the sidewalk in front of me. It was so tiny, so weak, so emaciated, barely able to walk, so I looked down and suddenly imagined this little vulnerable creature being flattened by the speeding cars roaring by in the street.

I found myself abruptly swooping up the little cat and carrying him to my flat. Little did I know the adventure that awaited me. He was in bad shape. His body raged full of lice, and his eyes were mostly shut. And he was skin and bones. I washed him, stupidly thinking this would clean up his lice. When I related this to neighbors who came to my rescue later, they cringed. "You never bathe a cat—it may freeze!" they warned me.

Sure enough, my new little friend was shivering from cold. I wrapped him in an old towel. I went next door to a small convenience store, looking for milk and cat food, not knowing that the owner was part of an underground, informal network of stray cat-helpers in the neighborhood. When I told her I had a kitten, she got excited and asked to see him.

She picked him up, and within a few minutes, she had a cardboard box for him to settle into. She brought cat food along with instructions for its use, and she told me about the nearby pet shop where I could get him a syringe to feed him warm milk. I'd been coming to stay in the neighborhood for years and never knew a pet shop existed.

The kitten didn't like the box, and when I let him out of it, he seemed to have a knack for rummaging through my shoes. That's when I named him "Papoutsa." One of my students in the study-abroad program volunteered to adopt the cat. That started us on another trail—finding a vet in the neighborhood, getting all the cat's shots, and preparing him a "Kitty Visa," so he could be taken to the United States. In a couple of weeks, he was flown there.

I saw him not long ago—a totally different cat. Huge, content, well-groomed, in paradise. Not all stray animals have such a happy ending. Pet owners in Greece who tire of their pets or can no longer afford them, simply drive to a park, drop them off, and drive away. Greece is full of strays. There is no neutering program. Few resources exist to help such animals. For the Athens 2004 Olympic Games, rumor has it that Greek officials rounded up all the stray dogs of Athens and put them in a holding pen outside the city. Then they were returned to the streets after the Games ended. It was an opportunity to neuter them, but this did not happen. You see them wandering the streets of major cities. Diseased. Unhappy. Limbs broken. Hungry and without love. There are many caring Greek souls who provide some food for them, but it is not enough to sustain them. A woman recently revealed four dogs poisoned in Crete. Man's and woman's best friend increasingly becomes a victim of the economic crisis A nation's true standing is measured by its ability to help its weakest members The strays of Greece deserve attention. Life and death? They live it every day!

Rebuilding Athens—Is Snooty Always Bad?

Ioannina, April 28

No one who spends any amount of time in Athens can miss the swanky district of Kolonaki.

Rising on the hill just north of the Parliament building, it seems a strange place to locate the Beverly Hills of Athens. It's steep, and not far from the chaos and anarchy of the "Republic" of Exarcheia. It offers no wide street or signature square to attract customers. Quite the opposite: narrow streets and a nondescript square that looks cheap and shopworn.

Kolonaki smells of money. This may be due to the plethora

of luxury cars visibly parked in the streets there. Or the Dolce and Gabbana-suited beautiful people hanging around its expansive cafes. Or the peculiar dismissive attitude of the financially well-endowed.

Since many foreign consulates populate the lower portion of the hill, it makes sense that their residences—not your typical hovel for such diplomats!—would stand in the same area. Kolonaki may strike you at first for its many shoe stores. Is there a serious shoe fetish in the area or are shops trying to take advantage of higher markups? These are not just shoes, but "shooz." Footwear as art. It's stunning to think that folks actually wear some of the odd models displayed, some seemingly designed by the Spanish Inquisition, but in fact they do. In abundance.

The economic crisis affected Kolonaki just like the rest of Athens and the country. But as the rents in the area took a dive, new entrepreneurs came in. This happened in other shopping areas of Athens as well. Nike, for example, signed a lease late last year for a store on fashionable Ermou Street off Syntagma Square for about half the previous rental fee.

Kolonaki makes a return with cute and innovative shops. There is The Dark Side of Chocolate at 49 Solonos Street that from one look seems only inviting to artistas and their hangers-on. But this little café brims with charm, even wit. You stare at its façade, and you imagine a young writer hacking away at the Great Greek Screenplay on the laptop. Or rather, iPad.

Carpo is another new addition. On the corner of Kanari and Merlin streets, Carpo seems more suitable for a shopping mall, but it somehow keeps its authenticity alive. It sells dried nuts. The owners of Carpo distribute nuts wholesale and have so for twenty-two years, but now they have decided to sell to customers directly. And it seems there are no better buyers than Kolonakistas. Some nuts with your Blahnik shoes?!

Whether it's a sign of the complete collapse of Western Civilization or a slide into further social decadence in a time of punishing national economic contraction, cupcakes are taking Athens by storm. There was a dance craze during the French Revolution, too! Freud may say something about this emerging phenomenon: meanwhile, we are left to ponder the cakes in two manifestations: Emi's Cupcakes at 7 Karneadou Street and Philippe Cupcakes at 10 Kapsali. Part of the attraction may be the simplicity of cupcakes, as well as their contrast to traditional Greek honey-lemon syruped desserts. I once ate an entire baklava in my village and was sick for three days. Not so with cupcakes, which seem to disappear in a flash.

I must confess I've not been a big fan of Kolonaki, even as I am strangely drawn to its faux seriousness and bland façade. Yet these latest incarnations may signal a new chapter in the district. After all, does anyone sell cupcakes in Beverly Hills?

Scent of a Nation—Aromas of Greece

Ioannina, April 30

Our nose impacts how we view and interact with reality around us. We all have memories of a particular smell triggering some thought from the past. I've had that feeling many times with smells from the Greek village where I was born.

I remember Paris because of the aroma of fresh baguettes and croissants cascading out of bakeries during early morning walks in the city. These stay with me even today. I know Seattle from the sea-salt smell of Elliot Bay. There is Los Angeles and the pine smell driving along Mulholland. In Greece, the smells are dominated by nature, except for those just outside a bakery or Zaharoplasteio (pastry shop). It's a flora's paradise here. Everywhere there are flowers and bushes and trees and grass that stimulate the olfactory glands to sweeten the experience of our lives. The jasmine with its sweet honeysuckle smell in the evening—especially on a hot summer evening when life begins after 9 P.M. The scent of oregano growing wild in the hillsides surrounding my village. The fresh smell of figs ripped open after being picked off the tree. The scent of "lisfaki," or wild mountain tea that grew on the mountains above the village.

These smells wafted through our noses and our consciousness, which made living in the village seem so sweet and memorable, despite the crushing poverty. I never felt poor, ever, perhaps because of such sweet scents around me. It was difficult when my family moved to Seattle—there are few aromas there. A sweet smell can put you at ease, calm you, give you a shot of tranquility that all of us need. The admonition to stop and smell the roses was not just for the act itself, but that the smell will remind you of the majesty of existence. It's also a reminder that this is a big life we live in. We are surrounded by so much nature, and it seems none more so than in Greece. News brings us disasters (tsunamis, tornadoes, earthquakes) but nary one has ever reminded us to stand under a pine tree in the morning when a cool breeze blows. Or sit by a beach in the late evening and let the salty air penetrate the imagination through one's nose. Or stand by one of those beehive-like outdoor ovens rarely seen in Greece anymore when freshly baked loaves of bread are removed from it. Do any of these, and tell me if they do not make life a grand experience.

We have glasses for our eyes, ornaments for our ears, gloss for our lips, lotion for our hands, but of all the senses, the nose stands unadorned, often ridiculed and the subject of plastic surgery. If you are very bored, find yourself a nice garden and sit in it for a while, preferably in the evening after the sun has cooled.

Look around the various plants and shrubs, and let your nose take over. Wisteria, gladiolas, irises, ferns, cyclamen, peonies, herbs, perennials, lavender, rosemary, pink rose, alliums, hibiscus.

When I walk around the campus of the University of Ioannina now, I am dazzled by the smells of the place. Shrubs and plants in full bloom. The red poppies visible in the grassy knolls. And everywhere the riot of smell that makes living here so special. It means following one's nose.

Media of Nations—Death & Elections

Ioannina, May 1

Here are the deaths:

38-year-old geologist hanging from a lamp-post in Athens.

35-year-old priest plunges to death from his balcony in Northern Greece.

23-year-old student shoots himself in the head.

Grim news and getting grimmer. Economic disasters always bring more suicides, but the news exaggerates the dramatic while skipping over what may be deeper causes of such deaths. The economic meltdown of Greece may be the last straw for some people already on the edge of life.

Suicide is a complex issue. It involves many factors: hopelessness, a grim sense that life gets worse, or the thought that it may never get better—these and many other factors go into what may cause a person to end his or her life. Our media-dominated society today harvests death and destruction, as agricultural society once harvested wheat and rye.

News media in Greece may heighten this as a way to bring attention to the coming national elections—letting the public know what is at stake in the choice for a new prime minister. Investigative stories that are deeper and more reflective in nature simply don't find the space or the time on news channels.

Death pervades our culture, but a particular kind of death—not the dignified kind but that which comes suddenly, unexpectedly, shockingly, brazenly, viciously. If we better reflected on suicide, we might realize that it's an act of desperation that marks an end point for an unhappy human being. We should feel pity. We should consider the impact of the suicide on the living relatives and friends. It is for them to pick up the pieces and go forward and live with the consequences of the suicide. Even as the human toll of the self-inflicted deaths in Greece rises, the figures are still lower than in Germany or Finland. While it is now 5 per 100,000 residents in Greece, it is 9 and 34 respectively in those two other European countries. Yet we don't hear stories about self-death in Germany and Finland. We only hear it about Greece because of its economic spotlight in the news. To break this awful news cycle requires that Greece get back on her feet. Then a different kind of story—a new narrative—will emerge. Grimness will be followed by cheerful stories. Success stories. Families working again. Economy expanding. More babies produced. Nightlife returning in Athens. Etc. Until then, we must suffer our calamities. We must bear the bad news. We must soldier through.

If only life were more balanced. Away from the media glare, it might be.

Historic Greek Vote Sunday!

Ioannina, May 3

You arrive at the poll station. A table is lined with stacks of photocopies of the slates from thirty-two party, coalition, and individual candidates. You collect sheets from many parties, and inside the booth, shove your single choice into the ballot box. This is how the voting will take place this Sunday in Greece. It's a monumental photocopying job and paper-recycling effort for the 20,560 polling stations nationwide. The 9,851,000 eligible voters will be joined by 360,000 new ones in the election. Then everyone sits back to see the results on television, starting at 9:30 P.M.

The two dominant parties ruling Greece the past thirty years—liberal PASOK (led by Evangelos Venizelos) and conservative New Democracy (led by Antonis Samaras)—have lost public standing. Support has bled from these two centrist parties and instead flowed to an increasing number of splinter groups—including the right-leaning Independent Greeks, left-leaning Democratic Left, and the neo-Nazi Golden Dawn.

Some tiny parties with interesting names will not participate in the election—National Hope, Friends of Man, and Citizens Assembly. This vote promises to be one of the strangest and most fragmented in decades. A chaotic political landscape may emerge, without clear direction, and a new prime minister may not be known for some time.

The election results may capture the chaos and anger in the country, channeling a defining moment in the nation's history. The credit binge that brought the country to its knees is over, and Greece searches its soul to find new ways to survive in the ultra-competitive marketplace.

What the election cannot and will not do is provide a vision of where Greece must go. Visions don't emerge from elections; they come from people. Politicians vocalize anger, but they don't offer a grand mission for the country. In ancient Greece, democracy was more than just voting—it was a quasi-religious experience. People participated in the affairs of the community because community represented the holy and the good. The community creates the means of achieving the good, noble life. It was a grand teacher that showed us how to put aside our petty differences and act in unison for the greater benefit of all. It brought different classes together in ways they rarely met otherwise. Not many regard democracy as holy today; quite the opposite. The drum roll of corruption rusts our thirst for involvement in politics.

We hate our leaders, we tire of the sloganeering, we turn away from the speeches. Democracy is more than just voting. It's thinking and debating and even arguing. It's taking stands, voicing concerns, and dissenting. Seeing the possible in the impossible. Doing things to help the community.

The slips of paper in a polling station are just a start. It's real, living, heart-beating human beings engaging with the world. Perhaps we need to reawaken the ancient Greek democratic model.

The National and the Personal

Ioannina, May 6

In these entries, I try to build an understanding of Greece that is deeper than the superficial news stories that hit us every day. Only over time and by looking at hundreds of newspaper or online stories can you start to see patterns and begin to see what we may gingerly call 'wisdom.' When news comes to us in bits, we cannot see the larger picture. That's the point, often. It takes a concerted effort to see what is really going on and not just the fragmentary pieces. This is what I am trying to do. I may not always be right, and I hope I am not, since that wouldn't be human. But at least I give you my perspective. It's not easy to make sense of the events in Greece. So much takes place now it's impossible to digest it all and spit out some larger view. The suicides, the corruption scandals, the political grandstanding, the continued worsening economy, it's hard to know what it all means in the larger scheme of life. It's like being on a boat rocked by wave after treacherous wave of turbulent water with no end in sight.

Are things getting better? Worse? Can the problems be fixed? Will a new national rebrand really help? Will starting new export businesses make Greece a better place? What about encouraging more study abroad programs to Greece? Part of me is sad about events taking place in Greece. It is not easy to see people you know being dismissed from work. They don't deserve it.

The other part of me witnesses something new, even though it's still chaotic and unformed. And that's the difficult part—how to describe this new Greece being birthed. What to call it? Greece is pregnant with something, but no one knows quite yet what it is. I hope to explain it to you when it does become more visible.

Personal details tell us a lot about the state of reality, the well-being of the people. What people are actually doing on the ground is more telling than a speech by a politician. It's easy to make a grand speech. The sidewalk is less appealing, but more honest.

Although thousands of Greeks now leave the country each year, looking for better economic opportunities elsewhere, this has been true for much of modern Greek history. What is less obvious is that changes are taking place in small and subtle ways. Store clerks are now friendlier than they used to be. Politeness is not the naive emotion it once was here. People see the value of being courteous to tourists. And everywhere is the feeling that the last chapter in this economic crisis has not yet been written. It is an extraordinary time to be here in Greece. In some respects, truly epic.

A Homer poem is being written by 10.8 million Greeks in modern dress.

New Greek Political Landscape

Ioannina, May 7

The biggest news to come from the national elections of 6 May 2012 is the stunning success of the neo-Nazi or Golden Dawn party—it received nearly 7% of the vote and looks to enter the new Parliament with twenty-one seats.

While the conservative New Democracy won the overall election with 19% of the vote, it was hardly a winning result. It was down from its 2009 total of 34%. Liberal PASOK fared even worse—its total of just above 13% of the vote in this election puts it at its lowest ever tally in any election. In 2009, it scored a victory with nearly 44% of the vote. Now the political jockeying begins as to who will form a government. And how.

Antonis Samaras of ND will have first crack, but there is also talk of a "Grand Coalition" of the left. Prior to the election, this Grand Coalition idea was floated by liberal Syriza leader Alexis Tsipras, thirty-eight, to other liberal parties, but few took up the cause.

More worrisome for many is the spectacular entry of the neo-Nazis Golden Dawn into Parliament. Their appearance on the Athens City Council two years ago caused conflict and hand-wringing. The party's intent is to provoke and disorganize. In the Greek media, Golden Dawn's amazing victory in the 6 May 2012 elections brought little discussion. The subject was generally avoided. The bigger story was the collapse of the two centrist parties. On Skai TV, the news anchors laughed and bantered over the election results but barely mentioned Golden Dawn. How this new landscape will play out internationally may be known in the coming weeks. It comes at a particularly awkward time in Greece's modern history, as it tries to throw off the shackles of a devastating economic tailspin while also trying to repair its national image.

How Golden Dawn will fit into this rebranding process is not discussed. On Sunday morning, a group of European Erasmus students witnessed a pitched battle between anarchists and Golden Dawn supporters in the central district of Thessaloniki. About twenty members from each group attacked each other, first verbally, then with rocks and Molotov cocktails. Cars were damaged as bystanders watched. No police arrived, and after about two hours, the battle died out at around 3:30 A.M.

At his victory speech, Golden Dawn leader, Nikolaos Michaloliakos, chortled at the national misunderstanding of his party. When members of the media covering the victory refused to stand when Michaloliakos entered, they were asked to leave. Behind Michaloliakos chillingly stood the red neo-Nazi flag—as if the 1930s had suddenly returned.

A new dawn rises in Greece, but not a golden one.

Neo-Fascism in Greece

Ioannina, May 8

About a year ago this feeling arose in Greece: chaos in the country needed a strong leader or "dictator." Someone to clean up the "mess"—runaway corruption, immigrants taking over central Athens, feelings of hopelessness, and the terribly itching sensation that Greece was unraveling at the hands of a degenerate or, at the least, uninterested political class.

It's now May 8, 2012, and Greece suddenly faces further political instability. The neo-Nazi Golden Dawn party charges into Parliament with 7% of the popular vote, or twenty-one MPs. That's about half a million votes. Nearly 35% of the electorate abstained from the election, a record for Greece. Even the Greek villages of Distomo and Arahovas, who suffered massacres at the hands of Nazis during World War II, also voted for Golden Dawn. In the 2007 election Golden Dawn squeezed only 0.29% of the vote.

The organization was started by Nikolas Michaloliakos after serving time in jail in the late 1970s for gun running while in the military. It was there that he met members of the disgraced military Colonels that ruled Greece from 1967 to 1974. There he learned the lessons the Colonels firmly believed: Greece is manifestly ungovernable and can only be ruled by a firm, punishing hand.

There have always been underground support for the Junta in

Greece; they fixed the economy—and got rid of long hair in men, pensioners today proudly whisper. Golden Dawn came to prominence during the Macedonia naming dispute in the early 1990s. A group of Golden Dawn toughs attacked a demonstration of anti-Macedonia supporters. The list of its acts stands in testament to their thuggery: attacking innocent immigrants, involved in shootings, beatings and other physical torture, and fighting leftists—it seemed often with the complicit help of Greek Police. It began with 200 hardcore members that had some connections with a neo-fascist party from South Africa.

In the 1980s Golden Dawn embraced neo-paganism, proclaiming fealty to the twelve Olympian Gods. Later they "converted" to Greek Orthodoxy. They also reject the Enlightenment and the Industrial Revolution. Party members prefer everyone to live on a farm and work all day for the Fatherland. Volunteers from Golden Dawn volunteered in the Bosnian War, and were present during the massacre in Srebernica.

In 2005 the party temporarily disbanded, but re-formed in 2007. Golden Dawn members often involve themselves in acts of football hooliganism. In 1999, during a match between Greece and Albania in Athens, Albanian supporters lit a Greek flag on fire. Greek media played up this event, which led to one Golden Dawn supporter going to central Athens and randomly shooting nine people. Two died from the attacks, several were injured and four are still paralyzed.

Amazingly, the group has some cachet within the bored, lascivious world of the Greek elite, particularly the upper-class offspring. Apparently, there is something stimulating about supporting an organization that takes the law unto itself. "They are men of action," I heard one daughter of a Greek Supreme Court justice tell me. Perhaps it's her way of upending the old world order, the one that held on to some traditions and values. That was a particular old, quaint world that seems boring to us today because it moved slowly, carefully, respectfully, and with a sense of generational connection. The youth today have little patience for such shopworn values. Retro-fascism, in this light, seems bold and daring.

It was the youth vote that pushed Golden Dawn to its present heights. A commentator called it the "Big Bang"—the youth that upended Greek politics. The centrist parties—New Democracy and PASOK—favored by the aged voters, were swept aside by the young who favored the leftist Syriza and Golden Dawn. Yet as one Greek resident told me recently: "Well, it's not like we are the only nation with a fascist party. Look in France, Netherlands, Denmark. And they get twice the votes that Golden Dawn got! So we're doing okay!"

In his victory speech after the election, Michaloliakos raged against the "pornographic TV channels" and those commentators who previously dismissed him. "The victory will continue!" he thundered.

Fate of a Nation—Seven Days in May!

Ioannina, May 12

It began with the elections on May 6, 2012, and ended with a hung Parliament and no government on May 12, 2012.

Seven days that changed Greece.

At the moment, the vultures circle above the country. With apparent chaos and instability, most commentators now expect the worst: Greece to officially default and leave the Eurozone this summer. Possibly even leave the European Union as well. Meanwhile, the troika (International Monetary Fund, European Central Bank and the European Commission) likely will pay a visit in June to check on Greece's finances, which worsen by the day. Yet underneath this chaos lies a crucial truth missed by many: Greece is undergoing a fundamental change in its political landscape. And this has deep repercussions for the future of Europe and the European Union experiment.

Greece has rarely been governed by a working coalition. The norm in Greek politics in its modern era has been single rule and no room for coalition governments. And two parties have run things—the conservative New Democracy and liberal PASOK—for the past four decades. Divided government has no real tradition in Greece. When it has come, it has spelled complete chaos (a Greek word). Greeks don't normally force their leaders from opposite ends of the political spectrum to work together. Yet this is how we can sum up the elections of May 6, 2012. The economic crisis changed past voting patterns, and this may lead to more consensus rule in the country. It was the youth vote who led the way—the eighteen- to thirty-four-year-olds who voted for smaller parties, unfortunately, including the neo-fascist Golden Dawn.

In a repeat election, likely in June, a more centrist vote may emerge. But the idea of coalition government remains. This does not obviate difficulty along the way. The political divisions in this country are real, lethal, and too ingrained to simply vanish overnight. It doesn't help that Greeks have long memories; they hold on to past evils and are too unwilling to let go of useless ghosts. In order for Greece to progress, however, consensus must happen.

The political splits—between the bourgeoisie and the rural, between elites and the masses, between its Ottoman past and its Western present—have muddled and burdened Greece with unnecessary fights and tension. These seven days altered this grim legacy.

For the first time, at least in the present era, major political parties spoke to each other—actually sat down in the same room and had a decent conversation, not just platitudes. Not across election speeches and Parliament debates. Not across press conferences and TV news interviews. Not across surrogates and press releases. Not through editorials and issued statements. Not through back-channel political maneuvering. Grudgingly, Greece is being dragged into the twenty-first century. Electorates across Europe increasingly call for more consensus rule in their governments. They know that divided governments force such dialogues; in effect, a checks and balances system.

The effects of these seven days in May may not be felt for a long time—often the way of history. Quiet steps taken away from the glare of the spotlight will in time have big repercussions. And from all this may actually emerge a strengthened, politically tighter Europe, which in the end is in everyone's interest—Greece's as well as Europe's.

Greece, Europe… Paralyzed?

Ioannina, May 13

A Greek communications professor once told me that you can tell a lot about a nation's soul by watching its TV news.

What does the TV news say about Greece? Watching Skai TV, Mega TV, or ERT News, this picture emerges: a lot of shouting, hand wringing, accusations, and very little consensus. Argumentative? It's often said of Jews that if you put ten of them in a room you get twelve different opinions. With Greeks, you might actually get more like fifteen!

The recent attempts to form a coalition government, thanks to the splinter votes of last Sunday's election, produced a lot of finger pointing by party leaders but no consensus. Worse, an apparent consensus reached by two party leaders on Thursday night was denounced the next day by the same leaders. In an extraordinary interview on Skai TV on Thursday night, two members of Parliament of the neo-Nazi party were interviewed. When asked how it was they supported the Junta that brutally ruled Greece from 1967 to 1974, the answer was as follows: "They had no debt."

In the same way, Adolf Hitler was often admired by many for providing wide, spacious roads and creating cheap Volkswagen cars. We are to accept cruelty because it can produce some benefits. By this measure, every madman and mass murderer in history can be condoned for merely doing some nice things. Kill a few million innocent folks, but if you can get the trains to run on time, you're okay. Golden Dawn will have twenty-one members in Parliament. They will be given offices, with staff and many perks—including immunity from prosecution. They can continue to physically abuse immigrants and its MPs will stand above the law. The connection between Golden Dawn, the police, and armed forces of Greece is particularly worrisome. In the Ambelokipi section of Athens, home of many police officers, 23% of the vote went to Golden Dawn.

A representative of the Pakistani community was on Skai TV on Friday. He spoke about the constant attacks by members of Golden Dawn. When a Pakistani man complained to local police about physical attacks on members of his community, he was told to set up his own vigilante group.

An extraordinary dereliction of duty by the police? One wonders what tax dollars are being spent on. If police can't keep peace in the community, why are they being paid? Greece heads for an election. What this will do to solve its problems is anyone's guess. It's true that neo-Nazis do not just plague Greece; we see their kind darkening the entire continent. What is particularly striking is Golden Dawn's thuggery, savagery, rudeness, macho venality, and unspeakable arrogance—not matched by other neofascist groups across Europe. And they seem to like nothing more than to increase chaos.

Europe faces a huge dilemma: to cut off Greece from desperately needed funds and to unleash the conditions in which a group of humanoids (I cannot call them humans—they do not deserve such a title!) spread their blasphemy across a helpless land, or to simply keep the Greek patient alive until he recovers and comes to his senses. It's an epic moment in Europe's history: let Greece go from the Eurozone and perhaps even the European Union, or simply shake its head and hang on for the turbulent ride.

Europe is paralyzed.

Airlines Dropping Athens Flights

Ioannina, May 14

The list is long and gruesome:

1. Delta stopped its direct flights between New York and Athens. This on top of Olympic (a Greek carrier) itself and Continental, also dropping direct flights between U.S. and Athens. Same for US Airways.

2. KLM reduced its flights between Athens and Amsterdam, eliminating its early morning flight from Athens to Holland.

3. Air Canada reduced its flights to Athens.

4. Thai Air, after thirty-six years of service, cut its direct flights between Athens and Bangkok.

5. Gulf Air no longer flies between Athens and Bahrain. Singapore Airlines chose Istanbul to be its hub in the region over Athens.

6. Czech Airlines, Ukraine's Aerosvit and Finland's Blue1 reduced their flights to Athens.

This is in part due to "political instability" and the country's "poor image." It was said that the "lack of flexibility in the prices of flight services" by Athens International Airport contributed to a negative flight climate in Greece's capital. This, coupled with the fact that the economic meltdown in Greece has reduced consumer spending, causes airlines to search for greener pastures.

Greek officials have turned their attention towards attracting visitors from Russia and other eastern countries. Yet the picture remains grim. Germans who once flocked to Greece are staying away in droves, no doubt in part due to the negative image the country continues to receive in the German press. For most of us, the reduced or cancelled flights may not mean much, but to the Greek economy where tourism represents the largest industry, it is significant. Retail sales continue to plummet and *Kathimerini* recently reported that 1,000 retail stores closed per week in 2012.

It would be nice to think the best, not the worst; Greece has tragically been through savagery before, and few doubt that somehow the nation will survive, even if it merely limps into the future. It's the sheer size of the pain that is worrisome—the political chaos, the unemployment, the hopelessness, the drop in industrial production, reduced salaries, capital flight, businesses leaving Greece and many able-bodied women and men joining a growing line of emigrants to other parts of the globe.

For me, the reduction in airline flights is a minor inconvenience—my regular flights in and out of Greece have been interrupted, and I can no longer fly to Amsterdam and then to Seattle on my return trip home.

The possibility that Greece might leave the Eurozone and return to the drachma also weighs on my mind. Can I continue to lead study abroad programs to Greece? I try to be optimistic, yet at times I regard the turbulence ahead and see it making my life as a study abroad program director quite difficult.

Sadly, it is now that Greece most needs people like me—to bring students into the country and to help, in an infinitesimal way, to keep the economy going. Yet it seems that I am a bystander unable to make much of a difference. I follow the news as much as I can, often spending hours in the evening watching the two Internet news sources—Skai TV and Mega channel. What I see is political chaos and a lot of shouting. Always shouting. The extraordinary arrogance by some of the guests is, well, extraordinary. Yesterday there was a member of Parliament from SYRIZA on Skai TV. Young and confident. Yet she blithely dismissed concerns about the effects of reneging on the memorandum agreement signed with the Troika (International Monetary Fund, European Commission and European Central Bank). She thinks Greece has the money to take care of her social obligations.

That line was last used by George Papandreou in national elections in 2009. It turned out to be a lie.

Courage on Display—
The Paralympic Games!

Ioannina, May 15

It's a strange fact of life that we can be at our best in difficult, challenging moments. In these harsh economic times here in Greece, I am reminded of an event that took place during the Paralympic Games in Athens in 2004. Most of us know the Olympic Games, few of us know the Paralympic Games that follow.

I volunteered for the Athens 2004 Olympic Games and after a two-year wait, was accepted to work in the media department. I arrived about a week into the Games because of a scheduling conflict back home. I was there to catch the last half of the Games, and it was truly a marvel. There were too many of us working in the media room, but it was still cool to be gathered with so many volunteers from so many different nations.

Yet it was the Paralympic Games afterwards that brought something new to my life. I asked to volunteer for these Games, and in due time I was given my credentials. From the start, the Paralympic Games seemed an after-thought for the organizers. More attention was paid to the Olympic Games and with those over with, little focus came to the Paralympic athletes.

Yet it was not hard to see the contrast between the two events: one huge, the other infinitesimal and barely visible. The pomp and circumstances of the former versus the authentic human spirit of the latter. If the Olympic Games were an organizational triumph, the Paralympic Games were an organizational nightmare. Every day I dreaded coming to work. What saved me was watching the disabled athletes performing. The men in wheelchairs. The blind women. Those missing limbs. Others with no hearing. And each time I watched I was moved. Greatly! It was the only time as an Olympics volunteer that I experienced athletes regarding me in my uniform and smiling at me. That never happened at the Olympic Games.

But one incident stands out above all. I was in the stands when a Ukrainian male athlete—big, strong, blonde, Hollywood-attractive, but deaf—who had just won a track and field event, appeared in the stands with his coach. His gold medal hung around his neck. He needed to pass a row of spectators in the stands to get to the other side. He went to the person sitting on the aisle, and using body language, asked if he could cross the row. Immediately the spectators and all the others in the row rose to their feet and let the athlete and his coach pass through. What got me was what happened at the end. Keep in mind that this man had just won a gold medal at these Games. After crossing the row, he turned and regarded all those who stood up for him. In an ever-graceful gesture, he clasped his hands together and silently, gratefully bowed to them all. They stared back at him, transfixed. I don't think in their wildest imaginations could they have expected such a gesture in such a moment. Moved, they bowed back. And with that, the athlete turned and walked away.

This image stays with me. It was a huge lesson for me in human courage and decency. The moment barely lasted a minute, yet its effects have lasted years. Fate may hand us pain and yet we can return it with dignity and humility. We can speak of the unfairness of life, yet we can transcend it with noble grace.

The true spirit of athleticism lies in the Paralympic Games.

Greek Elections, Euro Exit in June?

Ioannina, May 16

The cover of popular German newsweekly *Der Spiegel* said it all: "Akropolis, Good-bye—Why Greece Must Leave the Euro!"

Greece's membership in the euro since 2002 took place under subterfuge and cooked books. The current inability of the Greek political elites to establish a unity government to lead the nation exasperates European leaders, and many are now asking Greece to leave the euro. This leads to more money being withdrawn from bank accounts and to an already damaged Greek banking sector.

Greece is in serious trouble and the turbulence worsens. I can write about this horror with some reflection and distance—after all, my home is in Seattle in the U.S. But to say that I am not affected avoids the stark truth: all those connected to Greece are affected. I have led study-abroad programs to Greece since 2005. I started the Athens study-abroad program in the aftermath of the Athens 2004 Olympic Games. As a volunteer at those amazing Games, I was impressed by the organization and effort made to put on a world-class event, and it was there that I decided (inspired by the Paralympic Games) that I could blend my interest in education and my love for Greece into a program that brought American students to this beautiful land to be challenged academically, to grow as individuals and to become global citizens.

Those were days of hope and promise. Like many Greeks, I felt in the cusp of a new emerging Greece as I joined this new vision. I was very proud, and still am, by what Greeks accomplished during those Athens 2004 Games. But the dream in 2010 became a nightmare. I am not completely sure how it happened. Economists speak of unsustainable debts that finally came due, while others blame the political class for failing to create a healthier economy able to withstand global financial swings.

Whatever the cause, Greece now stands on the edge of a huge pit. Everyone points fingers at each other, or at the Europeans. The neo-fascist Golden Dawn blames immigrants. Perhaps even the stray dogs come in for some opprobrium. What few utter is how to get out of this mess. Without an effective government, decisions cannot be made and the economy withers. Jobs are lost and lives are permanently ruined.

It's the 1930s all over again. Can we now expect a World War III to save us? The change from the euro to the drachma may seem trivial, but it changes how we plan and organize our own study-abroad programs to Greece. We budget, for example, several months in advance. If the drachma is reintroduced, this means new contracts must be drawn to reflect the new reality. All our current contracts are currently written in euros. And since economists expect inflation to kick in as a result of a potential reintroduction of the drachma, it makes budgeting for any study-abroad program difficult to manage. For example, what if we budget 1,000 drachmas for a hotel stay for our students, but by the time the program comes along, the price increases to 2,000 drachmas—how do we make up the difference? This is only for our program—these decisions are multiplied several thousand times a day and on a million times greater scale for other businesses and financial transfers.

Should we consider moving our programs to Cyprus? No.

Rather than moving the program, we should embrace the triumphal spirit that produced the highly successful Athens 2004 Olympic Games. With more significance and more at stake now, Greeks need to take responsibility and seed the ground for a new Greece to emerge. We can wait for a new government, or we can plant the new government inside us all now.

New Interim Greek Government as Economy Worsens

Ioannina, May 17

On Wednesday, Judge Panayiotis Pikramenos was chosen as interim Prime Minister of Greece until elections on June 17th, 2012.

Pikramenos ("embittered" in Greek) is the President of the Council of State, the highest judicial body in Greece. He was appointed to the position in accordance with the Greek Constitution by President of the Republic, Karolos Papoulias. Educated in Athens, with post-graduate studies in Paris, the sixty-seven year-old Pikramenos is politically neutral. He heads a government of technocrats during a time of deteriorating economic conditions. Worries about Greece's fate in the Eurozone have grown louder since the inconclusive election on May 6th, 2012. Recently, it was reported that Greece's economy in the first quarter of 2012 shrank by 6.2%. It's also noted for the first time in the five years of recession that more businesses are closing than opening. Unemployment stands at 21.7%, one of the highest in Europe.

In another blow, the European Central Bank is reducing its infusion of liquidity into the Greek banking system because of a refusal by banks in Greece to recapitalize their system. The chaotic economic and political situation in Greece hangs heavily over the demoralized public. Recently, two men, forty-five and forty-eight, violently attacked a seventy-eight-year-old Dutch pensioner because they thought he was German. He is in a hospital recovering from a broken nose and jaw.

Worsening fears of economic collapse contribute to the continuing drop in Greek tourism, its largest capital industry. Many in the country liken the situation to the 1930s, prior to the Greek fascist regime of Ioannis Metaxas beginning in 1936. The neo-Nazi and once political fringe party, Golden Dawn, has recently emerged as a protest group that captured a stunning 7% of the national vote in the May 6th elections. Yet the biggest concern now is the increasing possibility that Greece will leave the euro. While European leaders like Angela Merkel of Germany and Francois Hollande of France defend Greece remaining in the Eurozone, other European elites see Greece's euro exit as the likely outcome of worsening political instability. It has even been suggested that Greece be removed from the European Union itself.

Greek voters consistently favor the country's membership in the E.U. and Eurozone. However, Greeks also voted for parties that at the very minimum prefer a renegotiation of the austerity treaties signed with the country's creditors. European Commission President, Jose Manuel Barroso, refuses any changes to the agreement. Many economists expect Greece to leave the Eurozone by the end of the year, with default coming earlier.

Calling All Artists—Greece Needs You!

Ioannina, May 18

The Greek soul is intertwined with art and culture. There is perhaps more art and culture per square foot/meter in Greece than in any other nation on the globe. It is time we put that art tradition to good use during a critical time in the nation's history. I suggest the following: All Greek artists, whether in Greece or living abroad, start a massive "artistic community project" to up-lift the demoralized people of this great nation. This involves art-ists going into the community to conduct their art—free of charge—for the benefit of the nation. This means doing im-promptu poetry readings in parks and supermarket parking lots. It means doing short, spontaneous dancing in metro stations. It means holding dance classes in public squares and inviting people to join the dance. It means holding impromptu movie screenings on sidewalks, or against sides of buildings in the evenings for the benefit of a local neighborhood. It means being creative in how artists reach people—but the goal here is to reach people. It means doing short mini-plays in small plazas.

By themselves, none of these events are unique—we've seen them before. But what I suggest here is to do them on a grand, epic scale—thousands of such acts done all around Greece for a few months. Suicides rise in Greece, and so too does depression, worry, angst, and other physical and psychological ailments. Maybe an artistic burgeoning can help raise spirits.

I don't think this has ever happened on this scale before, so I think it will garner a lot of media attention. In the process, per-haps it will be a bright light of sunshine amid the negative public-ity that pours forth from Greece on a daily basis. Some may believe that asking artists to donate their time, energy, and talent may encourage people to think of art as something free and freely available. I do not agree. Art is a valuable resource, a national treasure, and this is an emergency case. Greece suffers terribly, the worst since World War II. The act of artists coming to the rescue of a downtrodden people is to simply acknowledge the value of art itself. That no artist gets paid is because there are simply no funds available. Think of this as a goodwill gesture to help a severely strained community, the same way neighbors help each other when confronted by wild-fires or hurricanes.

This national economic emergency in Greece is as devastating as any shock nature can throw at us. This artistic project should start in the cities, Athens and Thessaloniki, and spread from there. This project should start immediately. No permits necessary. No bureaucratic approval. No time to write a press release. This is art serving humanity as it has done for tens of thousands of years.

And in the process, we change how Greece feels about herself.

Sweet Life of Ioannina

Ioannina, May 19

In ancient Greece, cities were the means not only of living a secure, more cultured life, but "taught" their residents to achieve the "good" life. City living was synonymous with good living. One discerns this principle in Socrates, who spoke of Athens in reverential terms.

I feel the same way about Ioannina. I came here for the first time in spring 2010 to do a study-abroad program with the University of Ioannina. My previous experience had been with such programs in Athens. The idea of coming to Ioannina did not appeal to me at all. The first month was difficult: the weather, a large campus, the distance from downtown Ioannina—all these contributed to a feeling of being isolated and withdrawn. By late April, the weather had warmed, and I found myself taking the bus to downtown.

We may think of small cities as rustic places, but they are more sophisticated than I imagined. In time, as I began to explore, I found an elegance and worldliness that manifested itself more and more. There is the main street, Dodoni, which cuts the city into two main parts. Along the way are quaint cafes and pastry shops, gyro stands, and trinket shops. There is the bakery shop at 47 28th October Street (that's the number 47 and the street called 28th October). The proprietors offer great muffins, cookies, spanakopites, and a variety of breads. They are fast, good, and efficient. No long chattering lines here. The periptero (kiosk) across from the "Diethnes" pastry shop on Dodoni Street (kiosks in Greece don't have addresses) is where I get my international edition of the New York Times that I share with my students—and for research.

A new discovery is a wonderful little coffee place called Bouka. It looks ultra modern, but it's also ultra friendly. Run by hard-working twenty-somethings, this place oozes charm and wit. Order a Greek coffee, and you will get it in the pot it was boiled in, along with a "loukoumi" dessert. It's a small but well-organized place. It has that Parisian touch to it.

You can always tell the soul of a place by the cleanliness of its bathrooms. Bouka's bathrooms are clean. There are plenty of places to eat in Ioannina. My favorite is a small taverna near the castle called "Ivi." It is the old-fashioned taverna—you see the food on display in the main counter, and you tell your waiter (and there is only one—a male waiter!) what you chose to eat. The place is clean, and the food is excellent: salads, fakes or lentil soup, orzo with meat, and pasta are just some of their specialties. Since it is also fairly cheap, I find myself eating there quite often. This is not Athens. The shops here tend toward the miniature—whether shoe stores, flower shops, or grocery stores.

The only exception is the elegant Grand Serai Hotel at 33 Dodoni Street: a big white elephant of a place that is also one of the best hotels in Greece, and in the current economic crisis, also one of the most reasonable. While it may look like something out of a Las Vegas casino on the outside, on the inside it brims with character and belle-époque charm. It's probably the best place in Greece to have a cup of tea. Just sitting in the lobby of the place makes one feel like a social elite. Pretensions can be addicting, and I find myself attracted to the place for that alone.

Ioannina will not attract many tourists, economic crisis or not, but it's a city one falls in love with even when you'd expect or wish the opposite. It's one of the few places that oozes natural warmth; the people are friendly, the atmosphere inviting, the pace of life endearing.

Remembering Civilization Lost . . . and Regained!

Ioannina, May 22

One of the best documentaries ever made was the *Civilisation* TV series originally broadcast on the BBC in 1969—prehistory for many today. It's available on YouTube, perhaps modern society's greatest invention.

In it, host Kenneth Clark, that great "stick in the mud," speaks to the essence of civilization—why we have it, why we need it, how we gain it, how we lose it. It's about the "vitality, order, energy and intellectual curiosity of human achievement." It's about hope and learning and confidence in the future. It's about feelings of permanence and stability and belonging somewhere in space and time. And consciously looking forward and backward and still seeing something of our humanity throughout. Does civilization still exist today?

If you think about the vast warehouse of "stuff" we produce—the gadgets, the gizmos, the videos, the technology, etc.— then I suppose we have a type of civilization. But is it the kind that deeply matters to our lives and makes us look courageously into the future? Civilization, for Clark, represents the human "as an intelligent, creative, orderly and compassionate animal." Its art is about harmonized proportion and human reason.

When I fly in a plane, I get this strong sense of beautiful proportion and technical reason, yet I don't get a refined feeling that a plane elevates me into a higher civilized consciousness. The truth may be that civilization as Clark defines it may sadly have passed. Our dreams today are captured by Internet entrepreneurs, financiers, sports stars, and actors, but few if any of these smug and pampered personalities devote any measure of their lives to advancing civilization. They do promote themselves, however, often at our expense. Clark warns us that civilizations are lost to fear, boredom, and meaningless ritual. Our peculiarly unfettered economies breed fear about our jobs and our security for tomorrow. And certainly, as a species, we are awash in boredom, chasing stories about celebrities' philandering ways.

And meaningless ritual? I see the candy displays at my local drugstore in Seattle being trotted out like dummies on a stage—the Christmas/Hanukkah candy replacing the Halloween variety, then those being replaced by the Valentine's display and then succumbing to Easter chocolate bunnies, etc. A never-ending cycle.

It's a strange fact of our civilization that we are awash in food, but we hunger for real nutrition. Much of our plentiful food is sugar-based, processed, chemically preserved, and of questionable nutritional value. But it's bountiful and cheap. Mars candy, delicious as it is, perhaps represents one of our culture's notable artistic achievements. Despite economic hardship in places in the Western world, we are better off financially than at any time in history. Today, the common person has gadgets that even the wealthiest human in history could scarcely imagine. Yet few of us care about our community and about the nature of its politics. We rarely get involved with anything in the neighborhood we live in that requires our honest commitment and energy.

We prefer to be independent agents—able to pick and choose our projects, our political parties, our friends, our lives. History gradually withers; no one seems to care what happened to human beings prior to 1991, the year the World Wide Web was birthed.

Our vocabulary shrinks; we speak the language of texting: C U, LOL and CIO. It's cute, in a way, even thrilling, but must it dominate our speaking? We yearn for something but don't know what it is, or how to get it. We are "imago hominis," the image of man, yet that facade is strangely empty and unsettled.

Here in Greece, because of the economic crisis, people are weary, confused, sad, angry, bewildered, overwhelmed, and desperate. Every day brings more shouting on Greek TV news. "The best lack all conviction," Clark quotes W. B. Yeats on the *Civilisation* program I am watching, "while the worst are full of passionate intensity." Can we regain our vitality and confidence? We can, and must, but it's not easy. The world turns eastward to China and India and southward to Brazil and Australia. But these societies, as brilliant and economically flourishing as they are, tragically follow our example: the rush toward materialism and environmental destruction.

We need to turn inside, to look within, yet we have lost our ability to reflect. We can build a new civilization based on environmental stewardship of the planet, but few seem inspired by this. If anything, it positively overwhelms us. Spirituality might play a role, if only the divine were truly alive for most of us. We can imagine a more tolerant world in people's perception of the Other, but we are too self-centered and afraid to get beyond our comfort zones, where differences are strength, not acts of war. It's possible to think of a new enlightened age with all our communication gadgets empowering us to rejuvenate democracy; but today, "people power" comes rarely and only under extraordinary circumstances.

In a mundane world, the information age calls for our subservience to corrupt, feckless leaders rather than calls to political action. We need a new civilization all right, but where and how it will come remains a mystery. Wait too long, and it will cease to matter. *Civilisation* the TV series tells us what we miss and what makes life vital—and what values we need to start civilization anew.

Neo-Nazis and Patras Youth Clash Against Police

Ioannina, May 23

Angry residents of Patras and followers of the neo-Nazi party, Golden Dawn attempted to storm an old factory in the city that sheltered a few dozen homeless immigrants.

Their anger was aroused by an alleged murder by an Afghan immigrant in a dispute with a local thirty-year-old resident of the area, Thanasis Lazaras. A crowd of males estimated between 200 and 350 tried to enter the site but were repelled by police. Clashes with police ensued, with a group of Golden Dawn supporters attacking a police officer on a motorcycle.

There were five injured in the melee, including two police officers and one Golden Dawn supporter. Police suspect three Afghan immigrants were involved in what became a fatal stabbing. There has been one Afghan arrest in the case. The clashes come amid increasing tension across Greece fed by growing anti-immigrant hysteria and inflamed by the neo-fascists that seem to thrive under such chaotic and turbulent conditions.

There have also been incidents involving attacks on immigrants in central Athens and other urban centers in Greece supposedly at the hands of Golden Dawn members. The deteriorating economy of Greece has angered many residents who increasingly vent their frustration at the immigrants who regularly pour into the country.

Many immigrants, including several hundred in the port of Patras, seek means to travel to Italy and other European countries. Their inability to do so leaves them stranded in ports like Patras, creating tension with locals. An immigrant group based in Greece reported today that several Patras residents attempted to break into the abandoned factory using a bulldozer. Images and video from the scene show pitched battles between hooded, dark-clothed youths and riot police. Rocks, flares and firebombs were thrown at police. It was also reported today that a group of thirty people attacked Golden Dawn Parliament member Michalis Arvanitis after an interview at a local TV station in Patras. The incident occurred after his interview at the Super B TV studio. He was set upon by the angry group, who punched him in the face and tore at his clothes. A reporter who tried to repel the group was also attacked. Tensions in the area remain high.

Greek Olympic Team 2012—The Real Winners!

Ioannina, May 24

It's a different Olympic Games for Greece this summer. The halcyon days of the Athens 2004 Olympics are long gone. Financial cutbacks earlier this year even raised the possibility that there might not be a Greek team at the London 2012 Games at all. Yet that fate was averted, at least for now. A team of 75 athletes will compete in London this summer, and while no one expects them to be barnburners, the fact that they will show up will be triumph enough. Our media focuses on the success stories—the gold medal winners, the improbable success tales, or the quirky narratives, such as the Jamaican bobsledding team. Courage is usually spelled out in terms of winner-take-all. It's a fact of all sports competitions, not just the Olympics—winners get all the glory. Less well known is that success can be measured by how far someone has travelled. If we always focus on the winner, we miss the point of real athleticism. The act of competing itself can be a win. A huge win.

Looking at the Hellenic Olympic Committee's website, one sees a brave face. There's a touching message by HOC president, Spyros Capralos, who acknowledges the difficult times but still claims a "particularly strong team." One of the possible stars of the Greek Olympic team is gymnast Vlassis Maras. He has put the economic hardships of Greece behind him, or perhaps he has it in front of him as a motivation to do well in London.

"My goal is to step up my exercise program and work harder," he's quoted in *Athens News*. "Once I get a few more things embedded into my repertoire, I think I will be able to compete with the other programs of the top athletes who will compete in London." London will be the third Olympic competition for Maras. "I'm a different athlete this time," he claims. He hopes to do much better than before, when he came home empty-handed.

There are other determined Greek athletes. Konstandinos Filippidis in the men's pole vault, and Sofia Ifantidou in the women's heptathlon are but two. Perhaps these will be names that suddenly pop into the media's radar, especially if they win. Rarely do we get inside the athlete's psyche to understand how far they have come just to get to the Olympics.

We rely on these metrics because they are the easiest to understand—you win a medal, or not. It's clear and evident and simple. A deeper interpretation is that just arriving at the Games may itself be a win for an athlete, or in this case, Greece's entire team in London. No one expects them to do well; how can they, when Greece seems daily to fluctuate between chaos and instability. The country faces another election (its first was May 6th), with the possibility that it may exit the Eurozone as well as the European Union itself.

There's even a name for this possibility now—"Grexit." For two weeks this summer in London, there may be a pause in the social instability. We will watch the Greek team enter during the opening ceremony and clap for their courage to come here even when circumstances suggested they should not.

The country that gave birth to both the original Games in Olympia in 776 BC/BCE as well as the first Modern Olympics in 1896 faced dissolution but somehow triumphed over the odds.

This is what the Olympic spirit is truly about. I hope we don't lose sight of this in all the pomp and circumstance of the Games. Triumphs rarely come finer or nobler than this.

Confessions of a Concerned Greek— Worrying About Evil!

Ioannina, May 26

My students and I were just in the beautiful town of Lefkada yesterday and we were appalled to find a bench in a public park spray-painted with the words, "Foreigners Out" by the neo-Nazi Golden Dawn party. And it was not just on this bench, but other sites as well in the town. It's not the first time I've seen neo-fascism on public display. The day I was on the campus of the University of Washington walking to take my Ph.D. exams, I saw a neo-Nazi flyer on the ground with the swastika on it. I was so stunned by this that I picked it up and took it with me during my examinations. So for the next two days, while I took my exams, that piece of paper stared at me from the bottom of the computer monitor. If I ever got tired during the test, I only had to peek at this odious slip of paper to renew my energy and my determination.

I lost three grandparents to World War II. I've never had a grandfather, or know what it feels like to call someone "Grandpa." That particular avenue in my life has been shut. Thanks to a madman named Adolph Hitler. And to think that there is a "legitimate" political party in Greece about to enter the Parliament that extols the virtues of Nazism sickens me to my core.

Seeding the World and
the Vanishing Jews of Ioannina

Ioannina, June 5

Their third-floor apartment lies on Josef Eliyia Street in the heart of what used to be the Jewish Quarter of Ioannina. It is now just another row of multi-storied apartment flats in downtown Ioannina. Up some stairs and suddenly you are in a small oasis in the middle of urbanity. After having toured the Jewish synagogue, the only remaining one in town, I wanted to come back from a special memorial service last month and sit with the couple I met there to discuss their work and passions.

Isaak has that New York Jewish energy, having been born in NYC, but the quick smile and warmth may be more Mediterranean. Diana shares his joy. They are both seventy. We sat in their long balcony and began our chat. I never intended to interview him, so I surprised even myself when I took out my reporter's notebook and started taking notes.

They are happy to be in Greece. It is their permanent home now. ". . . Although we may visit New York from time to time," Isaak adds.

What drives them is the work of "connecting families" as Isaak calls it—cataloguing and archiving family trees to help tie families that didn't have relations, had forgotten them, or simply didn't know they existed.

"I only charge when I have to do extra research, otherwise it's free," he claims. They both share the story of how they met in an acting class in Los Angeles. It was platonic at first; she was married at the time, but something about their time together seemed to elevate both.

Later, after she divorced, he called her in Portland, where she was staying. "We have unfinished business," he told her on the phone, inviting her to visit him in New York. So she visited him in the Big Apple. She met his mom and promptly "fell in love." From there, it would be the start of a beautiful relationship. After knowing each other for thirty years, they finally married. "It's been a beautiful life all along the way," Diana relates.

He talked about his research into how his family members, seven of them, were rescued by concerned Greeks. He even wrote a children's book about the experience. It was a long time before he met his family's rescuer in Israel, and like many such encounters, there was little dialogue and a lot of petting of the face. He suddenly jumps up and demonstrates with his wife's face.

I asked Isaak about the vanishing Jewish community in Ioannina. His face clouds. "Yes, there are thirty-two Jews in Ioannina. The entire Romaniote communities in the world, I mean, the Greek-speaking Jews who date from the time of the Roman and Byzantine empires, are a dying group. They have one synagogue in the U.S., six in Greece and two in Turkey. That's it!"

Tragic, when you think about it, he adds, that there were once 4,000 such Jews in Ioannina alone. He's helped many people in his life, partly out of desire to repay and honor those folks who rescued his family. Even when the FBI came snooping around his house looking for someone he was helping. "I used my acting talent with them," he quips. "I threw them off the trail." A happy man. Doing serious work. And Diana cheerfully there by his side.

Sexually abused by her father, Diana understands the role of the undeserving victim of oppression and evil. "'Why do you cry,' someone once asked me, and I tell him about what my father did to me and how nobody believed me when I spoke about it." No hint of anger or bitterness in her words. Somehow, she's made peace with it.

Isaak reminded us that there are two ways to deal with the world: "Patch the world up (which means do something about its problems) or seed the world. What we do is seed the world. Seed the children to create a better world!" I asked him about the worrisome rise of the neo-Nazi party in Greece.

"I don't think they will make inroads in Greece. So far they've not been violent. Graffiti but not violence. If Greeks can vote for a new government in June that can work with the European Union, this party will lose influence." Somehow, I got the strange impression that Isaak and Diana were human beings of the imagination. And it was proven to me by his tour of the back of what was once the Second Synagogue of Ioannina. We came upon a large courtyard. In coming to the spot, he asked us to imagine a building that, when the Nazis took it over, was used as a stable for their horses. "This insured it could never be used for a holy sanctuary again." There was much more to be said. I suspected this was not the last time we would see each other.

The Meaning of Greece

Athens, June 6

It is said of good actors that they know how to be "in the moment." It is a Buddhist concept; being able to fully immerse one's body, soul, and mind into a specific event—be it eating a meal, having a cup of coffee with a friend, watching a great movie, etc. Time ceases, and you are not worried about the future or the past; but rather you concentrate on the present, on what is before you.

Buddhists say the West is made up of a lot of human doings, not human beings. We simply don't know how to be here, right here, now, and enjoy this very second. Our culture forces us to always plan, always hope, always dream, in a ceaseless assembly line of expectations, and in the process, we let time—moments, days, weeks, months, years, decades, lifetimes—slip away.

Herein lies both the strength and weakness of the West. We

have produced the greatest material abundance, but our people are miserable, feel empty and lonely, jaded and cynical. Drugs and pills and alcohol fuel our happiness it seems; we are not able to simply stand in front of a field of grass and appreciate nature's grand paintings.

Money comes and goes, but time is irreplaceable. So what do we do with it? You can tell a lot about a culture by how its people spend time. Greece has a different rhythm than most countries. The heat forces residents to move at a slower pace than in northern Europe—it's a waste of energy otherwise. This slowed-down quality gives people the opportunity to get into the moment, otherwise impossible to do when in a hurry. If Greeks have a reputation of being lazy, it is only because they have learned (like other Mediterranean cultures) to save their energy for the evening, when it is cooler and friendlier to the human body. This explains why, when Greeks celebrate an event, they are fully engaged. In such moments, time freezes, and joy becomes the measure by which the clock moves. It is for this reason that Greeks are able to stare you in the eyes in a way that makes Westerners uncomfortable. In the West, we are not used to looking someone right in the eye—somehow it feels penetrating and even intrusive. Our sense of personal space is tighter than for most Europeans—and we take affront when someone breaches that space. In Greece, such a stare is a sign of deep respect—it is a way of showing another that you are paying attention, that your focus is entirely on that person. Ditto the distance between people. Watch how far apart Londoners stand when speaking to one another, then do the same with two Athenians—the Greeks are practically in each other's pockets. All these elements point to a country that is regularly in touch with its emotional needs.

This creates both challenges and unexpected moments of bonding. For tourists, the display of emotion in Greece is overwhelming—love and hate in equal measure. Visitors are stunned to see two people vehemently arguing, seemingly ready to come to blows; yet, in the next moment, they sit in a café and watch a football/soccer match together, laughing and cheering.

I use an ethnographic exercise in my classes to explain to my students this very concept: a Greek couple argue in a café, and it's starting to get ugly. Other patrons now hear the commotion and throw stares. Finally, as the fight seems about to get out of control, the man suddenly stands and tells his wife, "Would you like to dance?"

She regards him, at first stunned, but then relenting. They dance, and as they do, the emotion that drove them to anger dissipates, and they return to finish their meal, now enjoying each other's company. This could only happen in a Mediterranean country. It is hard for me to conceive of an American couple doing the same (first of all, there are few cafes in the States, and nobody dances in the middle of them!).

Despite all that happens economically, this part of the Greek soul remains. I thought of this the other day, as the heartache and pain of the desperate economy adds up: I opened my window and heard folk music playing on somebody's car stereo. In that moment, I realized that as long as that music plays, Greece will be okay.

Diaspora and the Eternally Nomadic Greeks

Chania, Crete, June 8

Over 70,000 Greeks have fled the country in the past few years as a result of the economic depression. (Today's announcement: unemployment rate at 21.9%).

There are two sides to this issue. The first deals with lives upturned, homes lost or forsaken, and friends and families separated. If anyone thinks it is easy to pick up your life and move to another country, please try it and come back and tell me about the experience. Even when the migration is for the best (leaving a war, escaping chaos, natural disaster, etc.), it is still not easy to let go of your home. We last saw this with the nuclear power disaster in Japan, when despite radiation and contamination, many refused to leave their premises.

We are geographically-bound animals, used to our homes, and this familiarity breeds comfort. To give it up is to abandon all the years lived in one place and the memories accumulated there. Few can do this.

When we left for America, I was eight, and I had heard all the stories about arriving in a land with gold in the streets. I took these tales as literal truth; no one explained to me they were metaphors. I knew the value of gold, so in the back of my mind I understood a principle here—we were leaving for economic reasons. Years later I would better understand the significance of our emigration—my family felt there was a better future for my brother and me in America. And indeed there was, when I think how my life would have been had I remained in Greece—probably a high-school teacher, married with three children, doing some writing on the side, staying away from politics, and clawing my way towards middle-class pretensions as much as I could.

This is the blessing of living in the diaspora; generally, life is better, at least economically. This explains why few diaspora Greeks return to the motherland. Attachments are also hard to give up, and it is here that the other side of the diaspora—sometimes hidden, sometimes overt—reveals itself. Wherever Greeks land, they seem to make a contribution to the adopted society. Doctors, lawyers, politicians, professors, entrepreneurs . . . they make an impact. This is true of many other ethnic groups.

What sets the Greeks apart is the insistence of family ties, on keeping back-home traditions alive. And here we begin to see the true value of the diaspora—when parts of the homeland are taken to the new land, enriching it in the process. These could be in the form of stories, art, poetry, archival material, or academic studies. There is a field called Diasporic Studies that focuses on the contributions and fate of those migratory populations. No longer can they remain hidden, these seemingly faceless populations, but now they are part of the fabric of the adopted land.

So what is lost and gained when someone picks up roots and flees to another land? Is there a net gain or net loss? This cannot be answered, at least not here, but it's a question worth asking and should be further explored.

Traveling in Greece: Through the Looking Glass Brightly

Chania, June 9

Here are my observations of Greece in the past few months living in this great country—in no specific order:

1. Bicycles. Suddenly there are bicyclists all over Greece—Athens, Patras, Olympia, Sparta, Nafplion—in a way I've never seen before. No doubt this is mostly due to the economic crisis and the rise in gas prices. But what a great and healthy new trend for the country!

2. Hotels are of varying quality. There are unexpected surprises, such as the truly exceptional Europa Hotel in Olympia, and sad and regrettably mediocre adobes such as the Asteria in Tolo that give Greece a bad name. Are there regular hotel inspections by the Ministry of Tourism to insure some semblance of consistency and order?

3. The drop in tourism numbers produces a certain desperation in some vendors that would be comical if it were not so serious. Food portion sizes have increased in the past year, in a ragged attempt to attract more foreigners. But these travelers

have only so much stomach capacity. Rather than turning them into human garbage cans, it is recommended to REDUCE the portions and focus on quality. Thankfully, some places took note of this suggestion—Dionysios in Sparta and the kitchen of the Alexandros hotel in Athens.

4. Deception. Why do some Greeks still think they can hoodwink travelers—do they think we're stupid? Our driver coming back from Lefkada saw a stricken car on the road and claimed it was his sister-in-law, so simply drove back without even asking us. When I quizzed him about it, he said it was actually his sister. Sister-in-law? Sister? As it happened, one of our guides knew the woman and said she is not related to our driver. Our driver was trying to "pick up" an attractive woman by helping with her car!

5. Examples of waste are everywhere: from the expensive turnstiles at archeological sites to unfinished roads that sit idle in the hot sun. This is not just a Greek problem, but a worldwide one, and this country, while deep crisis, needs to be careful how it spends its money. The government giving money to the professional soccer league is a terrible waste of taxpayers' funds.

6. We saw a demoralized people everywhere we went, yet they still managed to smile. Greeks have not yet lost their joy for life or zest for living.

7. A bakery with sweets made out of honey. Is this possible in Greece? There are so many "xaharoplasteia" in Greece that it's a shame not one of them makes desserts out of just honey. A revolution, this, if it were to happen.

8. I wish the Greek government would replace all the graffiti-laden street signs. Not only do they look bad, it's hard to read them sometimes. Easy to get lost.

9. Too many museums. Turn some of these museums into art galleries or teaching centers. Let non-profits run them.

10. Somebody should start a clean laundry company in various Greek cities where foreigners or tourists congregate. Who has time to do laundry when traveling?

11. One small thing that would help the economy—more businesses accepting credit cards. Greece is a cash society and this is not sustainable in our globalized economy. Taking Visa, MasterCard and Amex makes a lot of sense for businesses.

12. Let Greece be Greece. She will never be Germany or even France, but Greece can be what it always has been—a place to collect and enhance one's soul. Some new manufacturing industry would greatly help her economy, but the Greek soul will always remain, celebrating life rather than the pressure of work. Ideally, of course, it would be great to have both, but Greece has already chosen, so let's just go with that.

For me these past few months, I've felt a part of Greek history.

Europe and the Fate of Greece— A Rocky Fairytale!

Chania, June 10

It is unthinkable for many to consider Europe without Greece. After all, the name Europe itself comes from the Greek goddess Europa. Can Greece survive outside of the Eurozone and the European Union? The events that may lead to the "Grexit" are numerous and complex, and no matter what the experts say, no one really knows what the political, social, and economic costs are of leaving the Eurozone. Of more impact may be the psychological costs of Greece's exit. Psychologically, Greece belongs to the E.U., since its outlook is more Western than Oriental.

The mental temperature of the place locates it within a pan-European outlook—and I am not just talking about the middle-class lifestyle that exemplifies the European mentality here in

Greece. The middle-class lifestyle is not a European exclusive; we see this worldwide phenomenon now most tellingly in emerging economies like India or Brazil. What distinguishes the Western orientation of Greece's middle class is the pretension towards culture that, because of the Greco-Roman perpetuation of classical Greece that helped form Europe itself, connects the country to the continent. Those Elgin Marbles sit in the British Museum because it's still Europe, not Moscow or Beirut.

This explains why in recent polls, close to 80% of Greeks respond favorably to Greece staying in the E.U. and in the Eurozone. Cutting the tethers from Europe would bring Greece into a state of psycho-social paralysis. There was once an internal debate about where Greece belongs—to the Occident or the Orient. This debate hung heavily on the narrow shoulders of this little country, and with its entry into the E.U. in 1981, the quandary was seemingly resolved. Even with oriental elements and legacy, Greece still belongs to Europe. Leaving the E.U. would return this question to the Greek consciousness, and it would be regressive. It's like an adult with a sucker in his mouth.

With Greece out of the Eurozone and the E.U., the legitimacy of Europe would come into question. Some will surely say, well, Greece did not deserve to be in the euro club, and therefore, in the E.U., since it lied its way into it. There is truth here, in the same way that any new business cuts corners and takes moral shortcuts to become sustainable. If we dug deeper, however, we would find moral and economic lapses with German finances as well. And just about every other country in Europe. The European project was and still is designed to bring disparate elements together into a working whole. This was not done for charity, but for the real purpose of eliminating conflict and diplomatic strangulation on a continent that has suffered extreme violence, war, bloodshed, famine, political extremism, suicidal and social chaos.

We've seen shades of all of the above in Greece since 1940, and some, like social chaos, seem never too far away. If Greece leaves Europe, Europe itself exits Europe. There is no reason anymore to claim that the European project, this noble experiment, remains viable. At that point, the experiment is over. It would have failed.

In this darkest moment in the history of the European Union, cooler heads, and more visionary ones, must prevail. This is a tall order; Europe is mostly ruled by politically-correct bureaucrats, not individuals with any visionary sense of what must be done to relieve the current crisis. One must remain hopeful, even as many cling steadfastly to failure. Human events tend toward the latter rather than the former, but we can and do surprise ourselves. We sometimes wait for the barbarians, never realizing that the barbarians stare back from the mirror.

Qataris Buy Small Greek Island; Start of Invasion?

Chania, June 11

Oxeia is a boomerang-shaped island in the Ioanina Sea not far from the beautiful isle of Ithaca. It was just purchased from the Stamoulis family of Australia for a price of 5 million euros, down from the original asking price of 6.9 million euros. The purchasers were part of the royal family of Qatar, through their Qatar Holdings company.

According to recent announcements, part of the 1236-acre island will be developed as a resort. This despite the fact that the island, or at least a portion of it, is protected by the Natura 2000 designation. In normal circumstances, this sale might not raise eyebrows, but because it has taken place during harsh economic times in Greece, it raises concerns that the country will dump her islands to stay solvent. This sale was by a private owner, so the transaction has no direct bearing on the Greek economy, other than the property taxes it will contribute to the state's coffers. Will this now lead an invasion of others snapping up Greek islands? It has been known for some time that Israelis are interested in some of the Greek islands as possible sites for lavish resorts for seniors (closer than going to Florida).

For retired Israelis, the proximity to these islands could not be more attractive. They have a playground in their own backyard, which explains the recent warm relations between Greece and Israel. Will Oxeia's sale stoke further anti-immigrant sentiment in Greece? Hardly, but it might encourage other island sales.

The island that everyone expects to be sold belongs to Aristotle Onassis's granddaughter, Athena. The island of Skorpios, also in the Ioanian Sea, is valued at $200 million and has the likes of Madonna lined up to buy it the instant it goes up for sale. Its secluded harbor and virgin forest make it an ideal getaway for weary billionaires. There is something quite attractive about owning your own island. Being surrounded by water is like owning your own world. Once on an island, you can escape the gravitational hardships of modern reality.

It's almost a primeval desire: be commander of your own world while the rest of modernity rests out there beyond the waters of your island. Few of us get that privilege, but many of us secretly yearn for it. How often do we think of escaping the madness of modernity? Such fantasies today come with 5 million euro price tags. For us normal types, we must settle for a week's stay on Naxos or Lefkada.

For those who worry Greece will be overrun with billionaires taking over their islands, no need to be too concerned. There are over 2,000 islands in the country, more than the number of billionaires on this globe, so there's no chance all will be bought by the financial elites. More worrisome is the sometimes lack of appreciation for these islands. In some regard, Greeks take them for granted, and perhaps we should not blame them. If you live on an island all your life, it may be stifling. But there are not many island nations on earth (e.g., Indonesia, Micronesia, etc.), so they really are treasures to be appreciated. The hope is that the folks who bought Oxeia will share this concern and be good stewards of the island.

When news of the island purchase took place, I asked a local Greek resident about it. This was his reply: "Good for him. If I had the money, I'd buy all the Greek islands and not let a single tourist on them. If the European Union had the courage, they'd turn all the Greek islands into an environmental sanctuary and protect them from the hordes that tromp upon their fragile soil!"

Another resident was more sanguine: "Well, I don't know what to think. I suppose it's OK," she told me with a whimsical smile. A third was more neutral. "No opinion either way. People buy and sell all the time. I hope it helps the local economy. I hope it's not the start of an Arab invasion, but even so, if they can run Greece better, let them do it!"

Leaving Home—Long Time Residents Fleeing Greece

Chania, June 12

Greek-German couple Ioanna and Siegfried (not their real names) have lived on Crete for twenty years. They raised two children in that time and share a lovely "hacienda" style house, with garden, guest apartment, and a second living unit. It is a perfect place to enjoy the restful, quiet, bucolic life. They are both gainfully employed and have excellent relations in the community. I first met them last year, when my wife and I visited them during Easter. We sat in their veranda, spoke about the Greek political scene, and enjoyed a rather philosophical conversation.

When my wife and I made plans to return to Greece, visiting Ioanna and Siegfried was on top of our list. So it was with some anticipation that we visited their expanding home and sat for a superb, home-raised and home-cooked meal in the rear of the house. We spoke about the deteriorating social and political scene in Greece, and I wanted to find out how Siegfried being German affected their lives in the current anti-Merkel hysteria that has swept Crete and other parts of the country.

The conversation was at first rather matter-of-fact, although we spoke of the neo-Nazi party, Golden Dawn and their savage influence on the current social scene. Ioanna spoke about a patient of hers (she's a nurse) and telling how she met a little girl named Chrysa, who seemed sad that her name is now associated with the fascist party—in Greek, "Chrysi Avgi."

She tried to explain to the girl that Chrysi Avgi (Golden Dawn) refers to a beautiful part of the day and not to focus on the political party that has taken this name. The girl seemed somewhat convinced. "It was awful to have to explain to the little girl that her name was based on something so beautiful, while she knew it was partly ruined by these thugs," she intoned.

It was about two hours into the conversation that Siegfried revealed he and his wife are seriously thinking of leaving Greece. This was stunning. These two stalwarts of the community packing up and going?

"And where would you go?" I wanted to know.

"Switzerland," he quickly responded, as if not having to think about this an instant further.

A pall dropped on my heart, and I felt a bit sick to my stomach. She tried to laugh it off, adding, "No, we do not plan to leave Greece!"

He repeated about fleeing to Switzerland, and once again she laughed it off. How many other such conversations are taking place in Greece? Last week, the spokesperson for Golden Dawn threw water at another interviewee on television and slapped a member of Parliament who tried to stop him.

A few nights ago on the news, there were reports of Golden Dawn members involved in a fracas in Northern Greece. These incidents are real and may reveal a society coming apart at the seams. And here I must go back to the conversation with Ioanna and Siegfried.

These are decent human beings and contributing members of society. They have built a lovely home, they are educated and caring members of the community, and they love Greece. But how does Greece treat *them*?

When I asked him if he ever considered getting involved in politics, his reply was quick. "Can you imagine me speaking to politicians? I don't speak the same language as they, so how can I have a proper conversation with them?" He seemed sad and reflective as he cast these words into the air.

"Besides," he added, "can they accept a German in their midst speaking to them? Especially when they ask me how Merkel is doing, as if I have an 'in' with her simply because I'm German!" The evening was winding down, and we had spent three hours talking. I wish we could have continued longer, and in another time and place perhaps we could, but it was time to say good-night.

I trudged to the car. It was a long and silent ride back for my wife and me. Darkness had descended on the road. The same darkness, perhaps, that has descended upon Greece.

Athens—City of Staggering Dreams

Athens, June 14

It is 40° Celsius today here in Athens, or about 104° Fahrenheit. Eggs could hypothetically cook on the sidewalks, not that I'd like to test it out.

As I go about my errands, a sudden dream strikes me. Let's say tomorrow morning we wake up, and Greece's economy was booming. How would Athens be different? I began to imagine all those folks who left the big city for the countryside during the economic crisis returning back to Athens. Apartments suddenly fill up, and the streets are clogged with cars again. Conservation-minded folks give up their bicycles and return to their freedom-inducing cars. The center of Athens chokes with cars, and buses too, as tourists return in droves. Visitors had come during the crisis because of hotel and ferry discounts. Now they return, however, just because Athens and Greece are fashionable again. The *New York Times* does a few travel articles, the signal to mainstream society that all is well in this Mediterranean country. Along with the boom in tourism, there are new jobs in high-tech companies that settled in the Plaka area during the crisis years, because of cheap rents and great location, and now employ thousands—many of them are immigrants from the Middle East who wanted to be part of a European country yet still be close enough to fly back to their homes in Qatar, Iraq, United Arab Emirates, Egypt, etc.

As in any economic boom, the darker arts return. Prostitutes and the sex trade flourish in the back alleys of Syntagma, Plaka, Monastiraki, Omonia, and Thisio. So do the pickpockets and scam artists, who find easy pickings in the tourist overflow. Prices for meals zoom, and a village salad that once cost five euros, now is nine euros and higher. It is now nigh impossible to find a hotel. The Grand Bretagne is so full it resorts to giving rooms only to the most well-known and renowned. Famous rock stars with their fawning retinues and Doberman Pinschers suddenly are the only guests at the famed hotel. Limousines and Rolls Royces, hardly seen in years in Athens in the crisis years, now are spotted everywhere. Even in front of grocery stores. Out of these expensive carriages come homeless-dressed teenagers whose last names are bin Habin, Schapiro, Heidelberg, Smith, Bouquet, and Cilantro with the well-practiced smirks on their faces and spoiled manners that only cheap and vast wealth can endow.

Athens turns into one vast Stoli party—bars are everywhere—rooftops, basements, alleys, people's homes—and the alcohol flows like glacier water in spring. Few have any manners anymore; people are spotted fornicating in the National Gardens and genital petting—once rarely seen in public—now not only accepted but openly encouraged. People think: well, at least they touch each other instead of rioting as they used to do during the crisis period.

Those quaint grandmothers in black no longer exist; a government act forbids them from walking the streets of downtown Athens. Ditto the old pensioners playing backgammon in the tavernas: they too are not allowed to waste time on silly games. Police officers were retrained after the economic crisis and now have become social workers, rarely arresting anyone, but instead giving spot therapy to those causing infractions.

Speeding tickets are a thing of the past (there is even a police museum with examples of such old archival relics, including handcuffs no longer in use!). All police officers now retire at thirty-three, the same age as Jesus's death, the rationale being that young police officers communicate easier and better with the young that now populate the city.

The young do not want the old around; those old fogies remind them of death, and besides, these pensioners are ugly, urinate on themselves, and smell like wet socks. Marijuana? What flavor would you like, the young bartender asks in the downtown cafe.

Opium, speed, hashish, uppers, downers, crack, and other drugs are easily available, sometimes compliments of the local bank, to encourage new savings and checking accounts by the young.

Athens has turned into a mecca for these blissfully young. And the beautiful. And the apparently smart. And the sexy. And the financially able.

If you don't fit any of these categories, you're regarded with derisive laughter. There is no worse crime in this reality than being poor and polite and caring about your community. Prime Minister Alexis Tsipras, to thank all the young voters who swept him into office, regularly leads his bevy of huge, tattooed body-guards to Kolonaki, the most fashionable district of Athens, to hobnob with the youth vote, as he calls it, often drinking expensive cognac and sharing the latest Lady Gaga jokes.

For some, in this vision, Greece is considered the epitome of the democracy Solon and Socrates dreamt about. For me, I was choking with fear from what I imagined, and I snapped back to reality. I was in Syntagma Square. Marble was missing from steps and walls, from the riots of the past few years, but the place looked as it did in the past.

The tree where the pensioner shot himself is now marked by flowers and placards and anti-capitalist signs. I looked around, with downtown Athens staring at me. The city was worn, weary, tired, in need of make-up, but otherwise beating in its usual chaotic rhythm. Empty shops along Ermou visibly showed the economic crisis in action, but people still looked through the windows of stores still open, and some even carried shopping bags.

Grandmothers in black trotted in the streets. I let out a sigh of relief as we headed back to our hotels; it was just a daydream. The heat was unbearable, and the awful vision made it worse.

Election Blues—Greece on the Edge

Athens, June 16

Greece's parliamentary elections are tomorrow, Sunday the 17th. What will they bring? Some measure of stability? A new prime minister, perhaps New Democracy's old Sherman tank, Antonis Samaras, or SYRIZA's young Adonis, Alexis Tsipras? We can speculate, as everyone does in Greece, or we can simply resign ourselves to the fact that whatever government is chosen, it faces a monumental task. Greece is bankrupt. All claims about austerity measures do not hide this fact: the country has no money to pay wages, pensions, bills, etc., beyond two months.

Whether Greece stays in the Eurozone or not can be debated, but the outcome is uncertain and will be for some time. Banks, corporations, exporters that do business in Greece have prepared for the day when Greece returns to its old currency, the drachma, whose origins go back a couple of thousand years. Opinions of financiers and European bureaucrats are divided about leaving the euro.

The country governs only in the most basic sense; police do not respond to house calls and are not seen in the midst of trouble. In fact, they seem to positively avoid it. Society itself rules. Social exclusion and shame are the policing measures of the country. In many rural areas, police are rarely, if ever, seen.

Where do all the taxes go? Well, here's a partial list:

- Three cooked meals per day for students, weekends and holidays included, along with free books for students and subsidized housing.
- Money to the professional soccer/football leagues.
- Media campaigns to sell Greece as a tourist destination— with a new campaign each time a new government is elected.

- Money to singers for concerts to spread Greece's fame abroad, even though the concerts take place on their own.
- Subsidized routes for flights and ferries to serve specific islands.
- Building sports stadiums and halls that have little if any use after the opening ceremonies.
- Paying the political parties to maintain their staff.
- Underwriting all the expenses for 300 parliamentary members in a country of 10.8 million; compare, for example, the US: population 300 million and 535 legislators.
- Purchasing turnstiles at archeological sites that are never used and gather dust instead.

There is rampant tax evasion. Why does this happen? Here's one example that reinforces this reality. My friend owns property on Crete. Recently, the authorities decided to expand an existing road and took a portion of her property—a few square meters—to do so. Did the government compensate my friend? Not only did they not do so, but others whose property also was chipped away for the road expansion received no compensation either. They hired a lawyer and sued the state. They won. How much money did she eventually get for losing a portion of her property? Sixty euros.

When the government gives such little compensation, citizens wonder why they should give any of their hard earned tax money to the state. There are hundreds of thousands of other such examples. Can any government really tackle such problems? Change requires not just laws, of which many exist, but a mentality of enforcement.

All laws are undergirded by a willing and supportive population. When citizens refuse to heed laws, the paper such laws are written on might as well be shredded. A contract is not just a piece of paper but a promise to carry forth certain actions. When both parties in the agreement refuse to heed it, it has no value.

Greece badly needs competent leaders. It is a hallmark of all democracies. To survive and flourish, they must have great leaders on a regular basis. It is highly doubtful there has been a great leader in Greece since Constantine Caramanlis in the 1970s. Since then there've been a bevy of populists, demagogues, functionaries, and bureaucrats—no leaders of vision or clear idea of where Greece should go. If the election tomorrow produces such a leader, the country's bright future is possible. If not, Zimbabwe stands as the coming model for Greece.

What I Miss Most About Athens— Open-Air Cinemas

Athens, June 19

It is located on the cobblestoned pathway on the west side of the Acropolis. The main entrance is a throwback to modernity: a small box-office, posters of various films, all of them classic or near-classic, and an elderly couple chatting and invariably laughing with a customer or two. This is the Thisio open-air cinema. It was Wednesday evening, and the film playing was Alfred Hitchcock's *The Man Who Knew Too Much* starring James Stewart and Doris Day (1956). Such films end up on television in the U.S., brightly-lit 1950s films with perpetually smiling women like Day and avuncular males like Stewart who seem to occupy a world alien to us. And so it is. The irony, the double-entendres, and the sometimes lame jokes of the dialogue make one wonder if they were created for perpetually bored viewers.

When my family moved to the United States, I spent a lot of time watching such films on afternoon TV; it colored my views of America and the world. The impression it left on me was of an America deeply in love with itself but also caught up in a frightening world it wants to control. The dramatic tension comes from these two elements in perpetual war with each other. In the case of *The Man Who Knew Too Much*, this expresses itself in the innocent Americans abroad. We know this is a contradiction in terms today; no one is innocent anymore, but we put up with this convention for the sake of familiarity and because it makes for interesting entertainment.

Watching this same film in an open-air cinema, a different reality emerges from what I saw on afternoon TV: a much darker and more nuanced film than previously seen. In this new version, Hitchcock's classic reveals a strong anti-global tendency; all those dark-skinned folks are to be feared for their cunning and deception.

And, of course, in this world, blonde is good. Very, very good. Day can sing and smile and soothe and show all the stark emotions of dealing with a kidnapped son. The husband, James Stewart, is the usual laconic, mid-western Republican type: rustic sentimentality worn on the sleeve, and charm resting in his hands and jutting jaw.

Husband and wife move in an unstable world, not just their marriage but also that of Morocco and London. And what they gather is that their unstable marriage is far preferable to the sinister evil of that outside world. As we watch the film, we are surrounded by the fuzzy smell of jasmine that only comes at night in an open-air cinema in Athens. The stars are visible overhead. We are not constrained as in a closed theater but become part of the natural landscape.

This is the special experience of open-air cinema that has no substitute—and why film comes alive in such an experience. I doubt whether I would get a deep reading of Hitchcock's film in another setting, certainly not squatting in a room by myself seeing it on my laptop.

And it is here while watching this movie in the Thiseio openair movie house that I have an epiphany about my own life, about the moral compass of the world around me. Today, such roofless theaters are a rarity, even in Greece where they remain popular. Technology rules: convenience over having to drive to the theater, find parking, pay the eight euro entrance fee and sit with others around you, some of whom might be smoking and/or chatting on cell phones.

I always regard an open-air cinema event as two valuable hours in my life.

The Politics of Color in Greece
Athens, June 20

In the United States between 1880 and 1920, over 22 million immigrants entered the country, of which 450,000 were Greeks.

During that period, roughly 14.7% of the American population was foreign-born, the highest percentage in the nation's history. They came into a country that experienced deep convulsions about these new aliens, who looked, smelled, prayed, ate and socialized differently than previous northern, mostly Protestant European immigrants.

Greeks faced hostility wherever they went — beatings, intimidation, social exclusion, and even death. Nativists—born on American soil—resented the immigrants, even as they themselves, just a generation or two back, were once aliens.

It took a while for the melting pot notion in America to really take form; the idea being that the U.S., as a nation of immigrants, created the conditions for intermingling of races and ethnic groups. In practice, it was far more complicated. Greeks could be accepted in the U.S. for their food and colorful festivals; but, in social equality, they were decidedly inferior. Most prestigious jobs were closed to them. So they got into the restaurant business, or small retail, or in some cases, into the movie theater business.

They worked hard, pulled themselves up by their bootstraps, and now are regularly contributing members of society. In 1988, a Greek-American, Michael Dukakis, ran for U.S. President.

Greece experienced a net flow of immigrants, beginning in the 1990s when the Iron Curtain vanished and hundreds of thousands of Albanians poured into the country. No doubt there were some criminals among the influx of migrants. They brought crime and heartache to a lot of Greek residents, and in time, Albanians gained the reputation of being thieves, cheats, thugs, and even killers.

According to the United Nations, 971,000 immigrants live in Greece, half from Albania. This total represents 8.7% of the population. Their presence raised a dilemma in Greece's soul. As formerly a nation that expatriated hundreds of thousands to other countries, how did the nation now feel to be on the receiving end of a migratory wave?

Then other immigrants swept into Greece, many via the Turkish border in Thrace (northeastern Greece): from Iraq, Iran, Bangladesh, Pakistan, Afghanistan, Northern Africa, etc. All wanting work, and desperate for entry into deeper Europe (Italy the favored destination, with other places such as Germany, France, and England being preferred choices).

Like what happened with the earlier Greeks coming to America, the presence of immigrants raised the nativists' outcry. Last Saturday evening, two Algerian homeless men were beaten in Chania, Crete. Then early Tuesday morning, two men wielding sticks and metal crowbars attacked and severely beat an Egyptian man, also in Chania.

The Egyptian lies today in a hospital, his life under threat and missing a kidney. What takes place in Greece is not new. Many nations of the world have a sordid history of how they treat their immigrants. In the U.S., the infamous Ku Klux Klan rose up during the nativist hostility in the early 1900s as a racist bulwark against immigration and ethnic minorities. They intimidated many Greeks and made life for immigrants, including Catholics and African-Americans, pure hell.

The same bigotry is now on display in Greece, but rather than a social organization that does the bidding, it's a political party, one now joining the new Parliament, the neo-fascist Golden Dawn, that leads the battle-cry against the non-native to Greece. If not leading the charge, Golden Dawn gives thugs of all stripes and savagery in Greece dark cover to unleash their bitterness and viciousness on helpless victims. Even if they happen to be Dutch mistaken for Germans.

It may take a long time for this dark misery to finally be cleansed. Yet, there is no other choice. Such evil does not belong in any society, let alone one as culturally rich and historical as Greece.

Greece—Do You Ever Really Leave?

Athens, June 20

Leaving Greece is hard, leaving Athens even harder. While there is much to grouse about the city, there is still a certain undeniable charm.

Yet it is emptier than in years past, and the sense of dread about the coming election leaves the population increasingly on edge. As I came out of the metro station, the escalator was broken, so everyone had to climb the stairs one hot step at a time. I hear people whining behind me about this. Yes, this was Greece all right. Some things don't change. Folks here are so used to convenience that when something breaks down, they are hard-pressed to return to the old ways. At the same time, the elements that make this city livable and inviting still exist—the culture, the history, the landscape, the shopping—and will as long as there are willing participants.

In the end, my words mean little—only firsthand experience can tell the full story. There are infinitely more risks in doing so, but the rewards are infinite as well. We cannot simply live on the edge of some flat TV or computer screen. It's been almost three months since I arrived in Greece, and I leave now the same way I came—as one who remains steadfastly proud and enlivened by this country.

The people are still welcoming and generous, and the sense that anything is possible remains. Rules are not always pressed into laws, but often are flexible to accommodate real human needs. This is not always true of most nations. There is a dark side to this aspect, but the bright side remains—that this country exhibits humanity.

I don't think this element will ever leave Greece; nothing about the culture would allow it. Politicians come and go, and the sense of injustice about their governmental incompetence re-mains, but the belief that human beings still matter here survives.

What I take from this trip, what I always take from Greece is the bright hope that in the large scheme of things, life goes on. We go with it, if we choose, and that which stings us today may bring us roses tomorrow. Hope is born from difficult circum-stances; it also arises from a desire to think of tomorrow and its possibilities. I am Greek in the sense that I was born in a particu-lar place and time, but I am also made from that particular hope that is universal. I leave, I return, and leave again, and each time the rhythm becomes more organized and structured. My memo-ries stand outside of organization and structure, and they give force to that part of me that makes me human. And for this, I owe Greece eternal and honest gratitude.

No Miracle—Greece Loses to Germany in Euro Championships

Seattle, June 22

No war was declared. Germany didn't invade Greece. And no riots in the streets, either. Germany beat Greece fair and square on Friday in their Euro 2012 quarterfinal soccer match, 4–2.

The stronger, superior team clearly won. German Chancellor Angela Merkel followed the match in the stands. She was one of an estimated 15,000 German fans at the game in Gdansk, Poland. The Greek contingent could only muster 5,000 supporters; a smaller country, bad economy, and farther distance to travel all contributed to this tinier size. But all those topless Greek men in their warrior outfits sure made for a colorful show. From the opening whistle, the Germans dominated the game. Their height, muscularity, and mechanical supremacy overwhelmed the hustling and determined Greeks. Still, the Mediterraneans could be proud of the fighting spirit they showed on the pitch.

In the stadium, Chancellor Merkel had fun. The de facto leader of Europe jumped out of her seat like a teenager and showed the kind of emotion associated with Southern Europeans. Even the German coach/trainer was acting like a Greek politician in Parliament, waving his arms and gesticulating wildly.

The victory was sweet for Merkel. Only last Sunday did she celebrate her fifty-eighth birthday, so this win was an extra B-day gift. Prior to the match she called newly-minted Prime Minister Antonis Samaras of Greece to join her in the stands, but the Greek leader had more important things to do—namely, tackle the deep social and economic malaise that threatens to engulf his country into permanent chaos.

It was a touching gesture on Merkel's part to invite him; she was also the first world leader to call to congratulate him on becoming Prime Minister. She wished Samaras "the best of luck and every success in the difficult task he has before him," according to her spokesman.

For a few hours at the soccer/football match, Merkel escaped the hard decisions back home in Germany needed to save not only Greece but also Europe itself. The European Union seems on the brink of dissolution. Every day, the barbarians—otherwise known as bond traders—attack the thinning economic walls of Europe. Every day, those heartless greedy types with their fancy Armani suits and cheap sagging socks inch closer toward ruining the economies of not only Greece, but also Portugal, Spain, Ireland and even Italy. France seems next. How long before Germany itself comes under attack? What are Merkel's options to save a unified Europe? Daily calls from economists and lately the head of the International Monetary Fund, Christine Lagarde, say that some kind of eurobond and more central power for the European Central Bank are needed—solutions odious to the "Iron Frau."

But "Mutti," or "mother," as she is affectionately known to some, remains steadfast—the only solution is for profligate governments like Greece, Spain, and Italy to lower their expenses. Stop giving away all that cheap, euro-money to politicians' pet projects. It must be a pay as you go. No money, no project.

She grew up in East Germany under a communist regime, but her knowledge of capitalism is vast and deep. She's used to unpopular causes. But is she willing to stick to her guns at the cost of a divided and crippled, even dissolved, Europe? The answers to this and other impenetrable questions could not come from watching her team beat up on the resilient Greeks. The only viable way out of the current mess is greater fiscal and political union. In the end, it is one European family, brothers and sisters all.

Merkel will have to explore the most reflective part of her soul for a way forward to this monumental issue in the same way Abraham Lincoln looked into his before making the historic decision to create the Emancipation Proclamation in 1863 and free African Americans from slavery. It's a real-life game she has to win for the sake of Europe's unified future. Even the Greeks root for her!

Greek Prime Minister Scraps Private Jets

Seattle, August 27

Would you buy a used jet from Greek Prime Minister Antonis Samaras?

Greek media reported today that Samaras instructed his government to sell one of the private jets at his disposal and make another one available to the Greek Air Force for training as well as medical evacuations. Samaras will retain the Gulfstream V purchased for his official travels by former Prime Minister Costas Simitis, but he will also allow its use by the Air Force when he does not need it. The fleet's Embraer 30 will be offered to the Air Force while the Embraer 13 will be sold. It is unknown who will handle the sale or what limits there may be on its purchase. This follows an earlier directive by Samaras to close the restaurant at his official residence, the Maximos Mansion. This on top of salary reductions for all ministers in his cabinet.

Transforming Is Hard!

Seattle, September 5

No society that changes does so without pain and suffering.

Human history is full of examples of this, whether it was Greece after gaining independence in 1830 or the United States becoming a dominant world power in the late 1940s. What Greece suffers through now is nothing short of cataclysmic. The country is asked to let the old ways go.

A nation, a small one at that, where life was lived at a leisurely pace, is now being asked to alter itself and become a viable part of the global economic system. The days when Greece was known for 90% of its industry being run and operated by small-to medium-sized firms, often family owned, are done. The days when life could be lived simply, on a small yearly stipend, dependent on farming or husbandry, are over.

The time when working hard meant steady employment, are gone. Greece is being asked to become efficient as well as industrialized, using modern finance, with capital markets free and open to outside speculators. No more can this be a society based on middlemen or traders buying goods from one part of Greece and selling them to another, or importing them, adding duties and surcharges, then making money by having customers pay the added costs.

Today, thanks to the entry of China and India and Brazil and Russia in world markets, pricing is more competitive. You can buy it cheaper from China. So clothing isn't often made in Greece now. Greece must find other products to sell to the world market. But what kind of products? Olive oil and wine and figs can be sold cheaper by farmers in California, who use cheap Mexican labor. The only way to compete with them is for labor costs in Greece to go down. And that is what is happening. No one likes it, but is there a choice? Many folks in Greece resist change and they are right to do so. After all, it's not easy to see an old way of life die so suddenly and so thunderously. But since there is no real alternative at the moment, it seems Greece has to go along with the program, the bitter pill being forced by the nation's international creditors (the "troika"). It's sad to see this former way of life vanish before our eyes, taking with it long-held claims and views about reality. And replaced by a vision of life that is harsher, more capitalistic, more competitive, and less friendly.

The Danger Within

Seattle, September 9

Last Friday's (September 7, 2012) actions by a gang of neo-Hitler Golden Dawn thugs to demand the residency papers of street vendors who appear to be immigrants, and destroy their stands when they did not produce any papers, is a worrisome new chapter in the unfolding danger of this extreme political party. When any group in society takes the law into its own hands, there is no end it sight as to how far it goes. We can argue whether the police should have been doing the checking of residency papers of the apparent immigrants, but the issue here is not what the police can and should be doing. It's about a group of racists who have taken the law unto themselves and terrorize other human beings. The fact that small business owners in Greece fully support these discriminatory actions shows the extent to which Golden Dawn has penetrated into Greek society. Its seeds were planted many years ago. Removing those seeds will be a long and difficult process. This is the dilemma of the strong/weak state.

Greece has powerful social institutions that do not allow one to build and defend monopolies and cartels (strong state), but in social life exercise no power (weak state). The support of fascism by small-business owners is exactly the same support that brought Adolph Hitler to power. What amazes the onlooker is that the more criminal acts Golden Dawn commits, like last Friday's actions, the more popular and greater their support. This is the fantastic irony here and, of course this further encourages them. The organization of small business owners in Greece released a statement supporting the efforts of Golden Dawn and their actions to destroy vendors' stands as within their legal rights. There is a real battle taking place for the soul of Greece and right now, and Golden Dawn is winning.

When European Nations Collide in the Media

Seattle, October 10

Tuesday's visit by German Chancellor Angela Merkel to Greece set an interesting tone. On one level, it was a routine visit by one head of state to another. On another level, it was two nations witnessing the bitterness, anger, and recrimination of these past few years colliding in the media. Judging by what Reuters said, the reaction in German media by Merkel's reception in Greece was livid, referring to the Greeks as being "ungrateful." German media have been sharpening their knives against Greece for some time. We hear the labels: Lazy. Corrupt. Unproductive.

From the Greek side, there is the usual stupidity in protesters dressed in World War II Nazi uniforms, and even worse to see the media lapping it up. For Greek news outlets, Merkel's visit was a show of support for a cracking-apart Greece. They were grateful, despite some protesters who wanted to ruin the party.

The frenzy whipped up by German media and the fawning salivation by their Greek counterparts shows the extent to which news is simply a narrative of events. It's a story, told believably, but nevertheless a tale. History is less inclined to such interpretations, seeing the larger picture that we simply are too small to see ourselves right now. Europe changes before our eyes and it is unsettling.

Greece has lived beyond her means for some time. She got into the Eurozone in the first place by cooking her books. Yet slippery accounting is not just the purview of Athens, but takes place in a lot of European capitals. Most people believe that Greece will leave the euro. The only reason a bevy of European leaders in the past several weeks have flown to Greece is to avoid any post-euro guilt. They can sleep at night knowing they did all they could for Greece but in the end it was not enough. Greece's debt is too big. She had to go bankrupt. Better to use European money to save Spain's and Italy's bigger economies and not waste it on Greece. I believe Merkel really wants Greece to stay in the Eurozone. But she knows time is running out. The media storm surrounding her visit will die down, and we will be left facing the truth.

And the truth is: Europe is a deeply divided place, and any kind of United States of Europe is almost out of the question. As we inch toward war in Syria, we may soon forget what we were— twenty-seven E.U. nations in search of a union. We need each other, Germans and Greeks alike, but amid the shouting this message is lost. Merkel was in Greece to deliver it in person, to make sure it was heard. Too bad the media isn't listening.

Halloween? No, Just Another Scary Day in Greece

Seattle, October 31

In yet another stunning blow to sanity, the Eurogroup meeting today that was to resolve the issue of whether Greece should get the next tranche of money simply kicked the can farther down the road.

In a phone conference call between all seventeen members of the Eurozone, a decision was to have been made regarding Greece receiving the 31.5 billion euros it was due as part of its bailout package with international lenders. Confusion reigned as the meeting failed to produce a decision that must now be reached at the next November 12 meeting. The economic situation in Greece worsens by the day, with fiscal adjustments creating need for another bailout, perhaps to the tune of 20 to 30 billion euros.

The latest austerity measures that must be passed by the Greek Parliament for the country to finally receive the 31.5 billion euros is being rejected by leftist MPs. Already, the Democratic Left, DIMAR, a junior member of the coalition headed by Greek Prime Minister Antonis Samaras, indicated in the past two days that it will not vote for the package. The other coalition partner, PASOK, while its leader supports the package, may see its own members reject it. It's a harrowing time in Greece.

Turkish Prime Minister Recap Erdogan is in Berlin to discuss Turkey's entry into the European Union, putting pressure on Greece to exit the same organization. So the optimism of the past few weeks has turned into gloom, and a new term coined: "Grimbo," or Greek limbo. Some prefer the word "Grombie," or Greek zombie to explain the situation. Who needs Halloween?

Is This Greek Drama Nearing Act Three?

Seattle, November 1

We've seen and heard the term in many newscasts—"Greek drama" this, "Greek drama" that.

Think of the economic crisis in Greece and the words readily come to mind.

So how is the Greek drama in Greece doing? What act are we in? Is this play going to have a happy or sad ending? It began in December 2009 by then Prime Minister George Papandreou declaring that the country had no more money. This caught many off-guard, since only a few weeks before, he declared during the national campaign that Greece had plenty of money to weather the global economic downturn. Now current Prime Minister Antonis Samaras faces a similar wake-up call. He promised to his coalition partners in June that there would be no more changes made to labor laws in Greece. On that basis, the Democratic Left and PASOK, both leftist leaning, joined the coalition. But Samaras scuttled that agreement and in an attempt to pacify his international lenders, declared changes to the labor laws. Violating his own coalition pledges in the process.

So now Europe must decide if Greece deserves further financial help. Without that help, Greece is bankrupt come the end of November. If it's not Act Three, what is it? We near an end-point of some kind. The thought is that it will go down to the wire. When both sides face the abyss (and it is a deep one!), they will hammer out some kind of an agreement.

The Europeans will give more time to the Greeks and even more financial help, and in return the Greeks will speed up economic reform. All well and good. Until the next Act Three comes a few months later. And that's how this particular play will play out.

2.3 Million Greeks Living in Poverty

Seattle, November 2

Sotiris Nikos of *Kathimerini* today reported that 2.34 million Greeks are living below the poverty line, according to reports by the Hellenic Statistical Authority (ELSTAT).

The poverty line was set at 6,591 euros per year per person. Greece has been in an economic depression for the past three years, with unemployment at 25% and increasing. Over 1000 Greeks lose their jobs every day. For a nation of 10.8 million, the poverty rate is having a searing impact on social cohesion. Suicides, crimes and murders are all up. Socially, Greece may be suffering the worst since World War II. Some Greek residents resort to eating out of garbage cans.

Greek PM Samaras at Golgotha

Seattle, November 3

He is not the most popular man in Greece. He is caught in a hurricane of his own—his fragile governing coalition in the midst of collapse, while the Lagarde list affair (list of foreign accounts by wealthy Greeks to illegally avoid taxes) has the potential to engulf the entire political class of Greece and the people. The people seem on the verge of anarchy. Samaras at Golgotha.

The country he inherited on June 17 last summer is not the same as it is today. When he took over as Prime Minister, Antonis Samaras took the reins of a corrupt system that had been functioning more or less uninterrupted in Greece since the 1830s. The political class has always regarded governing as its private privilege. Those on the outside—the people who voted—are merely an abstraction. The real power sits with the few hundred Greek families that really control life in Greece. It is for these families that Greek politicos work. Not for the farmer in Crete, the dairyman in the Peloponnese, or the fisherman on Naxos. Nor for the millions of housewives whose daily work goes undervalued. What few realize is that society, civilization itself, is in the midst of a grand social upheaval begun by communication technology.

Television killed democracy in most nations it invaded; today, the Internet and smartphones are bringing it back slowly.

Samaras is a smart man but he may not be reading history well. He may think it's business as usual in Greece but the fact remains that corruption on the scale that has taken place for decades, if not centuries, is no longer sustainable. Not with 2.3 million Greeks living in poverty and 1,000 of them losing their jobs every day. Society can tolerate some corruption, but when it reaches a certain level, the bubble bursts. This is exactly what has happened in Greece.

And it was burst by a scruffy-bearded, stocky Greek named Costas Vaxevanis, who published the Lagarde list. The cat's out of the bag. It won't be put easily back. What is Samaras to do? Were he worth half his weight in salt, he would make hay of the Lagarde list and truly investigate the names on it. He would have a chance to start a new revolution in Greece—one that brings in fairness and justice. If the best information in Greece can only be obtained from foreign news sources, then something is wrong. This was true of communist countries. Greece is better than that and deserves more. As he trudges up Golgotha carrying the heavy cross, his crown of thorns turning his head into a mound of dried blood, Samaras must be looking at the other crucified victims ahead. But he has a chance—he is human, after all—to change the outcome.

Greece's new brand: "All time classic!"

Seattle, November 3

Greece's new tourism campaign targeting the global market, launched by the Greek National Tourism Organization (GNTO) under the slogan "Greece All Time Classic," was recently unveiled by Tourism Minister Olga Kefalogianni. "Greece is more than its current image," Kefalogianni said, adding that "crises come and go . . . Greece still is and always will be a strong brand-name." She also stressed that "restoring the country's reputation is the only choice that will allow our country to regain development and prosperity." Nikos Karahalios, GNTO secretary, reminded us that Greece still lists among the world's top twenty travel destinations.

Greek Parliament: Stepping into the 'Twilight Zone'

Seattle, November 5

It might be the week from hell.

On Monday, as reported by Reuters, the government of Prime Minister Antonis Samaras will deliver to Parliament the latest austerity measures needed if Greece is to receive the 31.5 billion euros due the country as part of its agreement with international lenders. Only about a week ago the measure was expected to pass the chamber. But late last week, a privatization bill that was a precursor to the austerity package barely passed Parliament. The Athens stock market plunged in panic selling as a result. It barely recovered on Friday, and only anemically. The real test is this week. Does it get any more tense than this?

If the austerity package, a source of friction and much tension between the government and its international lenders since at least July, does not pass Parliament, Greece faces complete bankruptcy. The country has been kept afloat by the help of the International Monetary Fund, the European Commission and the European Central Bank. Representatives from the three organizations, as well as European leaders, all visited Greece this past summer to let them know of the necessity of passing the austerity package. Samaras got the message. But it is not translating so well to Parliament. And now one of Samaras's coalition partners in his government, the Democratic Left, said it will not vote for the measures. This is a huge blow to Samaras, both personally and politically. And this past week it was revealed that the Greek economy, already shrunken by 20% these past five years, is in worse shape that previously predicted. And the budget deficit will balloon to an astronomical 190% of Gross Domestic Product in 2014. In short, it will rise to completely unsustainable levels.

Greek Parliament Approves First Step in Austerity Bills

Seattle, November 7

In a vote that pleased Greece's international lenders and saved the patient from being institutionalized, Parliament's economic committee approved the multi-bill presented by the government of Antonis Samaras. Last minute changes to the multi-bill were designed to win approval of the entire package. One such change involves not cutting benefits to disabled people, which Finance Minister Yiannis Stournaras approved. Another was a permanent fee imposed on shipping companies in Greece; in the original bill, it was to be "voluntary." It now goes to the full Parliament for a vote on midnight Wednesday, where it is expected to be narrowly approved. (The coalition government of Samaras fractured over the multi-bill, with junior partner Democratic Left indicating it would not vote for the measures.)

Greek Austerity and Budget: They Will Pass But at What Cost?

Seattle, November 7

It looks increasingly likely that the 500-page austerity bill and budget will pass Parliament. The latest efforts of Greece to continue receiving funds from its international lenders looks likely to pass in crucial votes in Parliament on Wednesday when the latest austerity measures are set for a vote. The 2013 budget is set for a vote in the same chamber on Sunday. The resultant multi-bills are a far cry from previous bills submitted to Parliament for passage. They will significantly alter the economic landscape in Greece - from allowing more flexibility to workers, which may mean grocery stores open on Sundays, to cutting the pay and pensions of previously untouchable groups (lawyers, judges, parliamentary staff, special police, Coast Guard, and intelligence officers). The voices in the streets speak a different tune. For them, this is economic suicide, and they protest their pay and pensions being cut. So far the demonstrations have been peaceful, but it does not take much to spark violence and chaos. Some years from now, Greece may be a different "now" than presently, but it must walk on hot coals to get there. How many can stomach such a feat? Yet in a democracy, their voices must be heard. It seems an impossible road. One cannot help but wonder at the changes taking place in Greece. Will they really yield fruit, or will the people finally reject them?

Chaos, Fighting, as Athens Protests Turn Nasty

Seattle, November 7

Peaceful demonstrations against the latest austerity measures imposed by Greece's international lenders turned ugly and violent this evening ahead of an important vote in Parliament at midnight.

Tens of thousands of protesters gathered in the afternoon and evening in downtown Athens to protest what they say is the gutting of people's salaries and pensions. Hooded youths broke out of the ranks and attacked police, who responded with tear gas, stun grenades and water cannons.

There were no injuries reported but running battles continue in the streets. In an unusual display, members of Parliament from the leftist SYRIZA party walked out on the precipice of the building overlooking Syntagma Square in sympathy with the protesters gathered there. They held a large banner against the lenders that read: "You destroyed the country, leave now."

Greek Parliament Passes
Austerity Bills in Close Vote

Seattle, November 7

In a wet, coolish evening, with 100,000 demonstrators packed cheek to jowl in Syntagama Square, Parliament debated the latest austerity package demanded by the country's international lenders. Without approval of the package, the lenders would stop further financial aid to Greece, now in its fifth year of a terrible and chaotic depression. But at 12:27A.M. Athens time, 153 votes agreed to accept the measure and with that, bond-holders and bankers and international observers took a sigh of relief. Even as the stock exchange in New York dove 312 points.

For Greece and Europe, it was a stunning if unexpected victory for a way out of the crisis. There were 128 votes against the bill, with 18 present and one absent. Greece squeaked through by the skin of its teeth, or whatever is left of it. Members of Parliament now take a much-needed rest until Thursday night, when they come back to vote on the 2013 budget. That vote is expected to be less divisive, but no less contentious. The real work begins now, Finance Minister Yiannis Stournaras tweeted to followers.

Europe Delays Greek Disbursement Until Nov. 26

Seattle, November 8

Greece did its part, passing a contentious and unpopular austerity bill in Parliament on early morning Thursday, as 100,000 protested in the streets, but the Europeans are delaying the next disbursement due the country under its second bailout agreement. The unnamed source claims the delay is due to a report that has yet to be delivered from the representative of the international lenders in Athens. Once the report is delivered, the Eurozone Group will decide on whether to release the funds or not. The delay may also be due to disagreement between the International Monetary Fund and European officials on how to further help Greece in light of worse than expected shrinkage in the economy and a debt level that will approach 190% in two years. This Sunday, Greek Parliament votes on the country's 2013 budget. The vote is expected to be a comfortable win for the coalition government of Prime Minister Antonis Samaras.

One Cliffhanger Down in Greece, Another on Sunday

Seattle, November 8

It was not the first cliffhanger in Parliament since the eruption of the economic crisis in 2009 nor will it be the last. But this morning's early vote to pass the multi-bill austerity measure may signal a significant shift in Greek thinking, if not its economy.

The vote cements Prime Minister Antonis Samaras as a forceful, if unpopular leader, willing and able to "get the job done." But it also shows the degree of desperation that Greece has fallen into. The multi-bill came after several weeks of haggling in which Finance Minister Yiannis Stournaras threatened to resign. That he didn't and that the vote passed by the slimmest of margins shows the way politics work in Greece. They don't. At least, not in any rational sense. Junior partners come aboard the government to help give it social legitimacy, but still can vote against bills (or at least abstain) out of principle. But even amidst the chaos there is a kind of symmetry not always found in other democracies: a willingness to sometimes throw caution to the wind and take a bold step. Now real work lies ahead for Greeks. And hard work. People suffer and they are scared. It's a difficult time to govern. But at least Samaras was not crucified. Not yet.

169

What Happens When Technocrats Argue Over Greece?

Seattle, November 12

An assumption about modernity is that technocrats are experts who know more than we do—know all the answers. As long as they have the requisite credentials from Harvard, Oxford or the Grande Ecole, they are light years above us. In the current tension between the International Monetary Fund and the European Union over how to get Greece's debts down, the falsity of this assumption is exposed. Clearly, the folks on both sides, technocrats all, do not have the answers or else we would not be having this discussion. The study of economics is not an exact science; if it were, our economy would run smoother and there would not be catastrophic dips in the global stock exchanges. The fact that we don't really know how our finances work gives us pause. The problem is: people's lives depend on it.

So now Greece stands waiting for help from Europe, but the firefighters can't agree where to put the water hose first, so the house burns out of control. We might laugh were the situation not so serious; but there's nothing funny about the current circumstance. Will German Chancellor Angela Merkel step in to save the day as she has done before?

Greece: New Playground for Rich Russians?

Seattle, November 22

The Greek Finance Ministry has decided that opening up the country to wealthy foreigners will help Greece's economy.

The riff-raff, such as those illegally coming into Greece, are being steadily rounded up and deported. But the red carpet is rolled out to wealthy jet-setters. The goal is to entice "high-income foreigners" (is it too difficult to say "millionaires and billionaires"?) from places like Russia by eliminating their income taxes from abroad. Only their income in Greece will be taxed.

Such a program is already underway in places like Switzerland and the United Kingdom, where several wealthy Russians have landed. This is a new approach for Greece and has some justification. It desperately needs wealthy foreigners to soak up unused real-estate, especially given the current meltdown in the housing market. It also encourages native Russians to evade their home taxes in favor of a cheaper rate in Greece. Apparently, Prime Minister Antonis Samaras and Russian President Vladimir Putin have already discussed such a scheme. It seems Greece will go by way of Cyprus—a private playground for rich Russians only too happy to dip into the warm waters of the Mediterranean.

But it's not just high-rollers who are invited to live in Greece. Anyone willing to invest at least 300,000 euros in real estate or a business will automatically get a five-year residency clause for themselves and their families. It amounts to a green-light for turning Greece into a special elitist resort. Meanwhile, those poor wretched souls from Afghanistan, Iraq, Kurdistan, North Africa and the like who come into Greece on rickety boats face growing police responses.

E.U. to Greece: So Close yet So Far Away

Seattle, November 26

As the European and North American stock markets took a small tumble today, there is still no word of a final agreement in the Eurogroup meeting to decide about Greece's next tranche of money it is owed under a previous agreement. This is the third time in three weeks that the Eurogroup of European finance ministers has met to decide how to lighten Greece's debt load and also disburse 31.2 billion euros in funds that are due under a past bailout agreement. They keep talking, keep crunching numbers, but no resolution comes forward.

Meanwhile, things are getting edgy in Athens as the government of Prime Minister Samaras awaits the final decision. Rumors spread earlier today that without the forthcoming funds, Samaras's government will collapse. A government spokesman vehemently denied the charge.

Greece Saved from Drowning

Seattle, November 30

Now that it's been a few days since last Monday's agreement was reached by the Eurogroup over the latest batch of money due Greece, we can see what a boost Greece has received. As many commentators have noted, Greece got an extra thirty years to repay back its loans. In other words, Europe took a haircut on the loans it has already given to Greece. That may not go well with voters in those countries that want Greece's head, but it is a practical and altogether smart decision. It also shows how much the Europeans want Greece to stay in the Eurozone. If there were doubts, these have now been dispelled. The E.U. would not keep funding Greece if it felt it was a lost cause. In the end, the E.U. family chose to save one of their own from drowning.

It came, however, with not one second to spare. Greece didn't just get a hand-out; it had to work for the money it got from Europe. If you consider the changes taking place in Greece, they are stunning and enormous. We may not recognize the country in a few years. As a friend recently told me, the fact that some people are now actually paying their taxes shows the extent of this change. Problems remain, as they always do, but it's heartening to see the changes taking place before our eyes.

The Year Draws to a Close

Seattle, December 1

The year is drawing to a merciful close.

After Antonis Samaras won the premiership, he formed a government with two smaller leftists parties—PASOK and Democratic Left, or DIMAR. It seemed an unlikely alliance, since Samaras heads the conservative New Democracy, between right and left, but it seemed to work in the beginning. The big task ahead for the coalition was the latest austerity package that had to be negotiated with the country's international lenders. There was a sense of urgency to the negotiations. Because the first elections in May proved inconclusive, the delay in negotiations also brought with it a postponement of Greece receiving billions in euros as part of its bailout package with the European Central Bank, the European Commission, and the International Monetary Fund. Rather than moving swiftly along, the negotiations became exercises in embittered hostility, with threats on either side being regularly made. Finance Minister Yiannis Stournaras threatened to resign, at least one time, but in the end—after weeks of haggling that would have impressed a vendor in an oriental bazaar—an agreement came.

That was in early November, just a few days before an important Eurogroup meeting was to take place on November 5th to decide about Greece receiving the billion euros owed it. The meeting came and went without a decision being made. It was postponed, awaiting the results of Greek Parliament's decisions over the austerity agreement.

The vote came in two parts—a vote for the austerity agreement signed between the Samaras government and the international lenders, and then another vote for the 2013 state budget. The first vote barely squeaked through, with 153 votes in favor while the second garnered 167 votes, thanks to the support of DIMAR.

A quiet disagreement that had been building up for some time between the IMF and the Europeans over how to effectively deal with Greece's debts blew out into the open at the moment when the country could least afford it. The immediately result was a further delay in its disbursement.

The underpinning of the argument was this: the IMF claims that Greece needs further funds to cover its budget shortfall, something the Europeans refused to countenance. While both parties agreed to give Greece two more years to gets its economic house in order, from 2014 to 2016, they disagreed on how to get there.

Epilogue 2012

There was a happy ending. The bailout agreement between Greece and its international lenders (International Monetary Fund, European Central Bank and European Commission) that was reached in Spring 2011 asked Greece for certain economic reforms. The lack of an elected government by Spring 2012 forced the reforms to wait. Because the first election in May was inconclusive, the second in June took place under dark clouds. As Greece headed to the polls, its coffers were running dry.

After New Democracy (conservative) leader Antonis Samaras was elected Prime Minister, the work of implementing the reforms began. That required negotiations with representatives of the international lenders. The negotiations got downright nasty and ugly. The Greek Finance Minister threatened to resign. Meanwhile, the state's bank accounts were seriously drying up. Negotiations that were supposed to be finished in summer dragged into the fall.

Finally, an agreement came in October. Then the Eurogroup (made up of the seventeen members of the E.U. who use the euro currency) had to meet to agree to the (concluded) negotiations. But rather than acceding to the terms negotiated, the Euro-group promptly got into a squabble with the director of the IMF, Christine Lagarde, over the nature of Greece's debt and how to best bring it down.

It took three meetings over three weeks to settle the issue, and it was partly settled. Finally, on Monday, November 26, 2012, the 31.2 billion euros due Greece earlier in the year were finally agreed to be disbursed. More important, Greece was given an extra thirty years to pay back its loans to its lenders. That's very much a haircut, meaning the European Central Bank and member E.U. nations will be taking a hit on their loans to Greece.

This might be considered bad news for the citizens of those other E.U. nations, but ultimately, it's good news for Greece. It was a moral boost that Greece desperately needed.

Meanwhile, Greece itself hung by a single thread. Its coffers were to be empty by the end of the November, meaning that there would be no payments made to pensioners, civil servants, and the like. Not paying these items would be catastrophic to the welfare and social cohesion of the country. But this was avoided at the last minute.

Where does Greece go from here? Many see years of misery and hardship, with no reason to think the country won't escape more pain. An economy that shrinks over 25% in the span of a few years cannot simply regenerate itself quickly. It takes time for people to come out of their protective shells and feel positive about their futures.

The fact that Greece's history has been riddled with tragedy provides some context to the present difficulty, but that does little to remove its pain and suffering, perhaps especially for the young generation, the so-called Lost Generation, those without decent jobs or decent futures. Greece's historical ability to survive tragedy means absolutely nothing to them. They see the fruits of their parents' and grandparents' lives—of cheap money washed up in Greece that did nothing to enhance the economy, but grow the people's debt instead—and realize they must pay for these horrible mistakes.

Already many have left to work abroad including Germany where tens of thousands have resettled. The hope that Greece provided at the turn of the twenty-first century vanished for them, and they must seek their future in other nations. This is the tragedy of the current situation—the extraordinary brain drain in Greece that will surely impact economic development for generations to come.

Countries, like human beings, age and change. At best, when we analyze or write about a nation, we simply capture a snapshot. It is not the final word. Reading these entries brings concern about how Greece will get out of this economic, social, and political mess. How does one simply get rid of an extreme neo-Nazi element in the country which may be deep-seated?

There may be some measure of hope. The attempt to "re-brand" Greece may seem deplorable, yet it is a way to jumpstart the conversation. If we can't reshape Greece in some fashion, at least in the eyes of the rest of the world, how will the country itself start to believe it can get out of its mess?

Someone might reply that the nation must first re-brand itself and then worry about how the rest of the world perceives it. Fair enough. But since no one seems to know how to do this, perhaps the outside world can intervene. If anything, this reveals how vital and important Greece is—that many care enough to want to do something about its terrible crisis.

No one doubts that Greece will survive in one fashion or another. The only question is how. It is one thing to live; it is another to live happily and productively. We all prefer to have decent lives. Given its sordid history of pain and suffering, the Greeks deserve this, too.

What can we learn from another country in deep crisis? Greece is in a big fat stinking mess: suicides, unemployment, and business closures surge, while pensions, salaries, and jobs evaporate.

The eighty-six days I spent in Greece were instructive. Most people seemed as happy and cheerful as ever, as I always remembered them, despite the economic woes, and even as residents desperately searched for work. Many have left for abroad.

It's another major Greek diaspora.

Underneath the smiles bubble worry and concern. And here lies the first lesson: life is never as great (or as awful) as we think it is. Our sadness may mask interior resilience, just as our happiness may hide deep angst. The Greeks don't hide either, and in that sense, I learned how they face their emotions more openly, honestly, and even painfully. Cafes and restaurants in the places I stayed seemed busy, and it was maybe due to this philosophy: as bad as things are, we can still go get a Freddo or a cappuccino and enjoy the beautiful scenery.

Then there is the Greek family. Greeks are very family-oriented, and while Greek families can be in each other's lives too much, they do look after each other in difficult times. This explains why even though suicides have risen by 40% in Greece, it is still fewer than the rate in Germany.

In crises, family members pool their resources. This may come in the form of lending cars to each other, helping family members find work, or giving a spare bedroom to a cousin who just lost her job.

Another valuable lesson is in Greek home ownership and its impact on the economic situation. About 80% of Greeks own their own home, higher than in the U.S. (67%) or other industrialized nations. Owning a house in Greece is like an insurance policy; no matter how bad things get, you always have a roof over your head. This Greek reality plays out in interesting ways. Because of the incredible 25% national unemployment rate, many

Greeks in the past two years moved out of apartments in the big cities and returned to their ancestral homes in rural villages. Even without work, with a house and some land, returnees can at least raise some crops and get by.

About 20% of the residents of Athens have left the city, if we are to believe current figures bandied about in Greek media. Many of these internal migrants are young and ambitious, and this creates an interesting new dynamic in village life once populated by pensioners and the aged. Suddenly, the young become farmers and bring their tech savvy with them, changing the entire ethos of the countryside. This change will no doubt play out in interesting ways in the future. For now, we can watch it and learn from it. Can it speak to a larger movement toward a more sustainable economy? Toward greater emphasis on agriculture and the environment as central pillars of a nation's economy?

These are questions left for the future.

2013

In 2013, Greece moved away from newspaper headlines, but its turmoil did not subside. In fact, even without riots and massive demonstrations, it lurched from crisis to crisis. I returned to Ioannina in Northern Greece during the spring and decided to pick up where I left off. I continued to write about the events in the country. Please note the new players on the scene, primarily the major part played by Greek Prime Minister Antonis Samaras since his election in June, 2012. He dominates the political reality, despite the growing opposition of leftist leader Alexis Tsipras, President of the very liberal party, SYRIZA. The two run neck-and-neck in opinion polls, and despite losing a member of his three-party coalition, namely, Fotis Kouvelas, of Democratic Renewal (DIMAR), Samaras continues to govern with the help of Eleftherios Venizelos, head of leftist PASOK. It's a razor-thin majority for a coalition in Parliament, but it's enough to just eke out new legislation. With the continuing rise of neo-Nazi Chrysi Avgi (Golden Dawn), the political landscape looks unstable. Matters will heat up and it's anyone guess as to where it will all end.

Day Three in Greece: A Bomb Goes Off

Athens, March 27, 2013

The explosion went off at about 8:30 P.M. on Wednesday night. I had just come back to my hotel room. I didn't know what to make of it; I thought perhaps it was some errant fireworks from the recent March 25th Greek Independence Day celebrations. I was too tired to think more about this, so I went promptly to sleep.

At about 1 A.M., I woke up again; the effects of jet lag hitting me. I surfed the net. That's when I saw the news report in the Greek daily *Kathimerini* about the bomb exploding outside the home of the son of a wealthy shipping magnate. It was the first time I'd heard an explosion in my life. It was an eerie, shocking feeling, an awful nightmare come true.

Like others, I am attuned to such carnage in war-torn places like Syria and Iraq. But not in Greece, not in Europe, and certainly not in North America. I wonder if I have been living an illusion this whole time and did not know it. I could ask the poor folks in London and Madrid who suffered terrible explosions in the past decade; they might share with me the same feelings of dread and horror. In the West, we live with an illusion of peace and tranquility, but reality elsewhere is far harsher.

I had just come back from a great interview with the founder of Zampple—a shop in downtown Athens that offers free samples to customers to try out new products—and feeling quite high about the future prospects of Athens. With the bomb explosion, I realized again the precariousness of life here, and I am not just talking about the economic crisis. Yet things are getting better, I am told.

And I've seen this with my own eyes—the flight from Frankfurt to Athens was absolutely packed. Tourists slowly trickle back. But with this explosion, we are reminded how much work remains. I hope regeneration can be accomplished for the sake of the great ideas and energy that flow around this great city. We can shatter our illusions, but not our hopes.

Thoughts at 2 A.M.

Athens, March 31

History moves at a glacial pace. We really live within two different worlds: one of the everyday, the mundane; and another we barely see. One involves our daily tasks, the other social change. We know the first, yet barely understand the second. And the mundane does a good job of hiding the historical.

In extraordinary circumstances like what is happening in Greece, two worlds collide and produce a unique glimpse into human reality. It does not take a fancy economics degree to realize that Greece is undergoing massive transformation.

Greece once rode on the coattails of Europe, taking all its benefits but being a fringe player in the process and not really returning much to the continent. Suddenly it is part of a new movement to reform itself, however painfully, to become a less secure, more competitive, more business-minded, more "globally-minded" nation. The old ways of doing business, politicking, even the way the country expresses itself through culture, must now become part of something larger, less friendly, more efficient, more inter-connected.

Greece is no longer Greece, but just another developing nation that must live in the twenty-first century. This new territory is well-trodden by the United States, Japan, increasingly China, Brazil, India, Russia and South Africa, and much of Western Europe. For a tiny nation like Greece, finding security in the larger European Union always meant being a kind of flea on a big dog called Europe.

But now there are too many other fleas, particularly the new E.U. members of Eastern Europe, and Greece is forced to carve out a new niche—one that has to look farther into the world of alliances. Hence Greece's growing involvement with China, for instance. Or reaching out to Israel. Or finding common ground with Qatar.

It's not an easy transformation. It's also one far more capitalistic than Greece ever knew before. And this is jarring. Greeks have lived in a kind of simple hut, a rather idyllic world. Now suddenly a ferocious neo-liberal wind has knocked it down and the people have to build a better house. Not with sticks but with cement and steel.

Where will it all lead? Likely to a more soulless society devoid of the simple pleasures that once adorned this great nation. But it will come with a more transparent and less corrupt society that will seem increasingly familiar to other countries of the globe.

Greece, with all its mighty history, will be another airport stop on the map, another pit-stop on the conveyor belt of an increasingly consumer-oriented life.

Still, as the economic crisis recedes, this massive metamorphosis will again find the mundane. The curtain will draw back on the historical transformation and be augmented by the quotidian. Life will seem rather "normal" again, but that will be an illusion. We'll be largely deluded into thinking that the everyday is what it used to be. But it won't be.

Albania on My Mind

Gjirokaster and Saranda, Albania, April 25 & 26th

The heat was already beginning to make my body uncomfortable, and it was barely 9 A.M. The bus chugged toward the Greek-Albania border, and my stomach always knotted when it came to this part of the trip. We never really knew what mood the border guards would be in; one year, we were forced to wait for an hour and a half because one student's American passport had not been stamped when he entered the country.

As always, it was our bus driver who led the effort. From inside the bus, I watched him go to the little guards' booth. I decided to venture out even though he explicitly told me to wait inside the bus. When I arrived at the guards' area, the driver told me to get everyone out of the bus, each holding his/her passports. Within a half-hour, we had all been let through. But there was the Albanian side now to deal with. We got back on the bus, drove about fifty meters and stopped again. How long will it take here?

Again, the same drill—we were to wait inside the bus, etc.— but as before, I decided to get out and approach the guards' booth. There was one guard inside and one hovering around. Our driver stood in front of the inside guard. There were some euro bills under the inside guard's nose, I noticed. By the time I arrived at the booth, the whole procedure had been done. That was it?

As the driver and I walked back from the bus, I asked him how he managed to get the whole thing taken care of so quickly. "Forty-five Euro," he replied.

How this bribe is determined is a mystery—why not 30 or 50, for instance? Why exactly 45? Do the guards accept anything below, say, 40 euros? Perhaps I should write an academic article just on this topic.

As the bus drove inside the border, we could see the differences from the Greece we just left. To American eyes, Greece is in that hazy area between developing and developed nation. There is no such gray zone for Albania. It is purely developing.

I pointed out the Greek villages perched on the mountainsides as we rumbled further into what was once communist territory. On the right I pointed out the bunkers that the great Enver Hoxha, literary critic, sexual innovator, romantic, whose day job was to run Albania as a communist paradise. He had a double, or sosi, to stand in for him at official functions when he was tired or bored; meanwhile, he stole money from every benefactor to his tiny nation (Tito's Yugoslavia, then Stalin's Soviet Union, then Mao's China), all the while boasting that the country never had any debt. Of course he never paid any of the loans back!

Gjirokaster is simply another mountain-side village writ large. It's a city, all right, full of Ottoman history and the five-a-day muezzin prayers.

But in my mind it's a village like the kind I grew up in in Greece. Without a developed economy, the emphasis turns to personal gossip and love passions as the currency of life here. Sure, the economy here does better than Greece's; at least, there's some growth, and the prospect of European Union membership has given the people hope (you can see the effects of this by all the baby carriages visible on the streets).

We were to meet some students at the University of Gjiro-kaster for our annual interview sessions. It's always a fun time for our students, and the Albanian students, too. This year was no exception, although this year I also noted more males participating than females. Was the word out that American women students had come and here was a chance for a ticket out of Albania?

The steps to the University of Gjirokaster appeared to be guarding a sacred temple, and seemed harder under the microwaving sun. We trudged up the stone steps as people's stares kept track of every tick of our bodies and smiling as they did.

I'm used to it, this being my fourth year, but I wondered how my students felt about it. Perhaps they loved all the attention.

At the top, we stopped and waited for our host to arrive to take us into the main building to meet a group of U.G. students.

We stood in anticipation of this meeting, one of the highlights of the study abroad program for my students. We are never disappointed and this year was no exception. They waited in beaming anticipation as we assembled in the room that in normal times was used to teach U.G. students Italian. The desks were arranged the old fashioned way; it reminded us of high school. Life is never fair, and the financial resources available are slim to none for this public university. After the courtesy speeches, we assembled with the students in a local café and they hung out with each other. This would last two hours while we met with both the Dean of Social Sciences and the President of the University himself.

It's hard to describe such meetings; this is 2013, yet it felt oddly like I'd been transported back to the Ottoman Empire circa 1850. Eventually, the students would head up to Ali Pasha's castle above the city, where a forlorn U2 American spy plane circa 1955 sits like a dying dog in the blazing heat. Lunch followed, and then the winding journey to Saranda on the Adriatic coast.

Saranda. The sleepy fishing village that became the Las Vegas of the Adriatic. Well, maybe not Vegas; perhaps more like commercialized Lynnwood, Washington just north of Seattle. Every year I arrive, gaudy new buildings have sprung up where weeds and deep-buried rocks once stood.

The main part of the town has not changed since 1492, but around the perimeter, especially south of the main harbor, it's a jumble I liken to old-Soviet-block-meets-Atlantic-City-charm. Lots of pinkish stucco and dreamy balconies. The dreams of some East-schooled architect with too much sherry to drink.

I would be thrilled were I less sensitive (or is it more?) but the bottom line is that being in the hotel is like living inside a Walgreen's window display. In my room, I could hear all the noises from the next one, and my balcony faced a partially finished house with a dog in the backyard that dragged around an empty plastic water bottle. Below me, the large heating oil tanks stood in the evening heat, and if I wanted to see the water I had to crank my head around the corner of the building.

I had to go for a walk to get my sanity back, assuming it's still there after years of doing study abroads. The main quay along the smelly harbor is a collection of bars, fast food joints (one proudly displayed this sign: "To do—Love, Dream, Be Free"), and trinket carts for the tourists. A wave of young people paraded on this Friday night; the usual display of enticing, aloof girls and testosterone-fueled boys. I know this scene from my own village back in Greece.

Some things never change.

I walked to the back of the harbor, trying to find something more real. I stumbled upon a pick-up football match at a small Astroturf field with players that moved in utter slow motion. Around me, overfilled garbage bins reminded me that refuse collection problems are not limited to Greece, or New York for that matter.

I'd seen enough. Back to the quay I dragged my slightly overweight body and parked it on a park bench with the other old-age gents staring at the cruising humans in front of us.

Evening threw off her lavender scents despite the strong salty-cum-plastic odor emanating from the beach beneath us. Baby carriages paraded by, confirming for me what I saw in Gjirokaster—Albania is hot for babies. In Greece, the population shrinks; here it expands. Which has a brighter future?

I lowered my head. Time to go back to the hotel, to nurse whatever pretensions I have that I know anything about this or any other place. My future is past; the big dreams that once sustained me are crowded in that overfilled bin back there.

Yet here in Albania, maybe they still hope and dream. Maybe in this pool hall of a place they still know how to raise families and build real futures. Maybe it's built on vice, bribes, stealing, drug running—I've read all the stories—but at least there's a future. Nobody has told them that Europe knows better. Nobody has put them in financial shackles and removed whatever aspirations young people once had. Funny, once Albanians risked their lives to get into Greece; now they risk their lives coming back.

The World of Meteora

Meteora (Greece), April 29

Meteora always held some special magnet for me, like a familiar park or a favored café. A place comfortable, known, easy, meditative, personable. And so it was that I woke up with anticipation. Peeking out the window, I could see the rising sun, not a lick of clouds in the glistening sky, brooding mountains staring at me like statues. I should have known it would be a hard day from the start; my run early that morning was ruined by a heaving, thuggish bus that drowned me in carbon monoxide. I was hoping for a longer run but it was not to be (I should be thankful; I still had my legs at the end of the run, not so the amputees at the Boston Marathon—and I was saying earlier that bombings in North America were barely thinkable).

Running back to shower, I managed to get some breakfast, but I was late to prepare for the bus ride with my students. How much this civilization runs by the clock, I lamented. How many billion watches are there in this world? Our bus never showed up. After some frantic calls, another bus was secured. Meanwhile, I realized it might be a good time to stock up on chocolate (I remembered being told by a parent the secret to soccer coaching: chocolate!). I saw the monster bus in the distance, but it passed our road and continued up towards the hospital. That must be our bus, I reckoned. I ran after it, eventually catching up just as it was backing up.

A few minutes later, we were heading on the main Egnatia freeway towards Meteora. When we got off the freeway to take the winding, potentially side-sliding turn-off, I knew this was not going to be a normal ride. I warned my students at the start of the bus ride about the nasty switchbacks, yet here I was, the one getting sick. Dang! We stopped for a bathroom break, and I took advantage of it to get some fresh air. It didn't help. Our driver, a sweet man but with a kamikaze speed fetish, seemed determined to make up for lost time. I kept my eyes glued to the front, avoiding any thought of food. Maybe it was the cheese that did it, I kept telling myself. Yet in no time we arrived in Meteora.

Meteora is a collection of spooky, awe-inspiring rocks with magnificent monasteries squatting on top. In another time, another space, monks and nuns lived on top of these dizzying places for the benefit of their souls and for God. The last century saw to it that marketing and tourism changed the picture slightly: the God of spirit replaced by the God of mammon. Guess who won.

First, the Grand Monastery that induces vertigo-like dizziness. Our female students donned wrap-around skirts, our males goofy sweatpants that looked new. "Fashionable!" one of the students grinned. I gave the students a tour of the main chapel, warning them to be respectful (only for one to release a particularly juicy foul word).

At least my stomach felt better; maybe it was the clear, chilly air; maybe it was the chapel; maybe it was just feeling like a bird above all humanity on this high perch. We started to leave as a crush of teenage Greek students engulfed the place.

St. Stephan's monastery, really a nunnery, is better in my book than the Grand Monastery, but when we got there the gate was closing on us and we had to leave. It was siesta time. OK, let's go eat; the students were getting hungry and no use waiting for two hours.

We had to ask some townsmen and two policemen where to find this big, boxy, communist-era large "cafeteria" with nice tables and not a single customer in sight. A fawning waiter greeted us at the entrance with a half-cocked smile. On the phone when I spoke to the organizer, we'd been promised salads, appetizers, and meats for every four people. But we were seated at uneven tables; the four of us "admin" types and the driver separated from the students. We did not get as many dishes as promised, I soon discovered.

I knew how the drill works: in Greece, you are promised one thing and delivered another, and the higher "class" the restaurant, the more likely you will be ripped off. Salads came to our table, and we wolfed them down. Then some petas, cold beans, and stuffed cabbage in extra creamy sauce (this is always the tip-off of a rip-off joint: the smothering of sauce on food that needs only a little). I expected a lot of food, but we got little. Meat came, and that completed the meal. I looked around the cavernous place; a music stand and several speakers indicated a lot of "fancy" weddings, baptisms, engagements took place here. At such occasions, bad food goes down better; plenty of wine and drink, music, dancing. None of these frills were available for us, so we had to face the wretched food face-to-face. I was being swindled before my eyes and could do nothing about it; the arrangements had been made back at the University and I could not change them. I imagined the conversation on Monday. "How was the meal?" I would be asked. "Terrible," I would reply, and watch as her face dropped precipitously. She would stop thinking about the terrible food and instead be ashamed that I questioned her arrangements. The meal was worth 120 euros, not the 280 we paid. We finished and went back to St. Stephan's. The gate was open and sinister-looking teenagers streamed out of it; they looked the type to kick a homeless person and laugh about it. We went in and found our way to the look-out point. A nun sprayed weeds in the area with pesticide; from a distance she looked like a mechanical fly released from a cheap sci-fi movie.

We left and were back on the road. Another day, another excursion. I wanted to be uplifted today; instead, I had been driven to near vomiting on the side of the road, wondering if life held any better career options. In a little while on the bus, I was asleep. When I woke up, I saw three speed-limit signs at the side of the road, two saying 70 and one saying 80. Some road construction person's idea of a roadside joke? We arrived back at the dorm, less uplifted and more in need of rest. In my mouth, the foul food hung with a bitter after-taste. MSG, my tongue told me. I was now back in my room but I needed a soda, so I debated whether to go downtown, yet thinking myself too weak to do so.

I managed to lift my butt off the chair and take the bus downtown. As we approached the center, I noticed some police and then, up ahead, a small demonstration by communists.

On a Friday night?

It was the usual collection of spike-haired misfits, Stalinists eggheads and second-hand-clothed ideologues. You see them on every Greek university campus; they eat the free food and spout about a workers' paradise. By now I had lost the need for a soda. I got a newspaper, some more bus tickets and headed home. The demonstration headed the other way, and soon I was back in my room. (I am lucky; back in Boston everyone is indoors as the manhunt for the second terrorist continues.)

Ioannina, Greece, May 1

Friends had told me about a small monastery not far from Ioannina, and it being Easter week, I thought I'd take the morning to check it out. It rests on the hillside like an eagle's nest, worn a little on the edges but still carrying spiritual dignity. I decided to stay behind for some needed rest while my students trekked up the trail to visit it. Then I imagined what possibilities might have greeted me had I decided to go there. I imagined the following conversation between me and a monk.

The Monastery of Predictions

The head monk had been watching me coming up the narrow trail to the monastery. He knew some English (as I found out when I'd telephoned him) so I expected to have a decent conversation. Sometimes my Greek can't be trusted, though, for it's still village Greek and many regard it with distaste.

We exchanged pleasantries, walked down a hallway to his office not far from the main sanctuary. He sat me down at a table while I imagined this office going back centuries. He had some fruit and sweets on the desk and kindly invited me to try them.

He asked me about the study-abroad program and about America in general. I gave him the usual banalities: why we come every year, attempts to educate a few students, the love of "patritha" (country), etc. He listened attentively, like a good therapist, but I never felt I was being judged.

"Do you really like Greece?" he asked me after I gave my thoughts about the U.S.

"What do you mean?" I retorted. "Isn't it obvious?"

He smiled. "I am not sure. You speak of Greece with a heavy heart. I was just curious."

I lowered my head a bit, so perhaps I was hiding something when I did not intend to. "Well, yes, there's a part of me that's sad about the current situation here."

"What, the economy, or the politics?" he asked in perfect English.

"Both."

He smiled again. "It's a two-headed beast and it's been with us for a long time."

I regarded him, a little bewildered. "What do you mean?" I asked, now my turn to be the inquisitor.

He smiled yet again. I realized that every time his lips broke into a grin, there was something behind it. "This country has never been able to properly feed itself nor police itself from the beginning of time. Why did the ancient Greeks establish colonies? Just to have new summer homes? No. This land has never been capable of giving us food. So we've always had to leave. Look what's happening now. As for politics, well, we invented democracy. You know why? Because everything else we tried didn't work. But even democracy failed us!"

He stopped and reached for an apple, Red Delicious I think it was. He continued: "So people now seem so disappointed, or surprised, or feel helpless. They claim they read their history in school but if they did, none of them would be crying in their milk as they do right now!"

I could sense some anger welling up inside of him. In such moments, I know it's best to just let the anger flow out and not interrupt. I nodded encouragement. His eyes now took on a look of laser-like intensity.

"Of course, many blame God," he continued. "It's not their fault, it must be God's. Of course, God doesn't say anything back but simply takes it. What else can He do? What would you do? But I laugh. Tend to your own garden I tell them here, but who listens. The other day I had a young college student tell me I'm the oppressor, that the Church is the cause of all the economic problems. 'It doesn't pay any real estate taxes,' he said, 'and controls too much property, and the priests get paid by the government when they should be paid by the communities they serve, just like they do in America and most countries in Europe.' Fine idea, I told him. But if our salaries stop getting covered by the state, will he start paying tuition for going to the university? Oh, no, he didn't like that. Education should be a right of all people. Yes, I said, so should God. Why should one be free and not the other?" He took a big bite of the apple.

A strange silence fell in the room and I looked around the office, seeing his vast collection of books. I noticed that not all were in Greek.

"You seem like a well-read man," I sputtered, trying to fill the void.

"Many of them are gifts. I try to read but I don't have the patience any more," he replied.

"So, what do you do all day?" I asked.

"Not much. Eat a little. Sleep a little. Tend to the chores around this place. Sometimes I have a helper come in. Other times it's all me. We have some gardens and fruit trees in the back. There's always something to do."

"Family?"

He shook his head plaintively. "I gave up on that a long time ago. Who wants to marry an old codger like me?" (First time I've heard a Greek use that term.) "You?"

"My wife is back home. She teaches at a university. We don't have any children."

He nodded. "Do you miss her?"

"Very much."

"Maybe you should stop coming here and stay with her."

"I thought about that."

"Don't think about it. Just do it." He smiled. "Isn't that what Nike tells us?! The new God!"

He regarded me, taking another bite of his apple. "You know, God died in the last century and I wondered if He had been replaced by anything. For a long time I thought nothing had replaced Him, but recently I realized that's not the case."

"Really?" I wondered.

"Really. Nike is the new God. I know that sounds kind of silly, but it's true. They represent the lifestyle of today's youth. It's all about sports, and physiques, and sex, and having fun, and athleticism. No one ever talks about decency, morality, altruism, sincerity, charity, forgiveness. All those are gone!"

"Are you sure? Not everyone worships Nike."

"Ah, but enough to make a difference," he asserted.

"So, what're you saying? Should we all just live how Nike tells us to live?"

He grinned, and a deep thought swirled in his mind. "The jungle has always been with us from the time we left Africa. The only difference now is that it's dressed up in fine clothing and comes with sweet cologne. Freud was right—we are just savages. God was created to tame the savageness, but with God now dead, well, what's the point."

"Father, I am surprised to hear you say that," I countered. "Here you are a man of God and yet you're telling me that your boss is dead. That's not a very comforting thought."

"Tell me where's it's written that I have to provide comforting thoughts?!" he blasted back.

"Well, doesn't the Bible say that we are to love one another and forgive one another?"

"Yes, it does say that but it doesn't assure us that anybody has to accept it. And when they stop accepting it then they stop accepting God. That's their choice. That's their will. And God can't do a damn thing about it!"

He said it with such finality and even hostility that I realized it was no use arguing. How did it end up that I was defending God and he was denouncing Him?

"OK," I said after a few uncomfortable moments of silence. "So, where do we go from here?"

"Nowhere. We go nowhere. Here is Greece, it's just the same spinning of the chaotic wheel as before. Now you have those sick thugs at Golden Dawn spreading terror and madness across the land, yet each day they gain more and more support."

"Even within the Church, I understand."

"Church?! That's only a small part of it. They practically control the army and the police. Even politicians, ones you'd never think would ever dare to support them, do. I'm talking about leftists and liberals—they support the neo-fascists. And do you know how many businessmen support Golden Dawn? Thousands. I'm talking about wealthy, powerful businessmen who run big companies. It's incredible!"

"Can anything be done to stop the neo-fascists?" I asked.

"No. The whole madness must run its course, like what happened before with the Junta. There may be a coup one of these days, and Golden Dawn will be right up there in charge. And then we'll get bombed by the Turks and that will be the end of that. And in about 40 years, they'll come back again. Same can, different restaurant."

I looked at my watch. We'd been talking for a couple of hours and I could see he was getting visibly tired. I asked him if I could come back and visit him before I went back to the States and he smiled. "The door is always open to you. Come when the spirit moves you."

As he led me to the front door, he grabbed a small bag of loukoumia for me to try. "Just a small sample to make life sweeter for you."

"Thank you, Father. You have been most kind!"

"Nothing," he retorted. "If I ever come to America, you'd do the same."

As I trudged down the small trail, I wondered if I would indeed come back. What would we talk about? What more is there to say?

Easter Epiphany in Ioannina

Ioannina, May 5

The night always seems darker in Ioannina. Perhaps it's the rangy mountains that surround the city and envelop it with a thick, rocky blanket.

My students and I marched down to the bus stop to take the inter-urban to town. We would go to the midnight service at one of the churches there. I kept an eye open for a taxi, knowing that a bus might not be coming on a Saturday night and sure enough I was right. I hailed a taxi and in no time, we were in the main central square.

Empty. Devoid of human life. Few cars were parked on the road, as if the whole population had suddenly left town en masse.

We walked to the little church off the main square. It too was empty; a few souls sat in the chair inside and three priests chuckled in a small room off the main sanctuary.

"What time does the service start?" I asked them, apologizing first for interrupting them.

"Eleven," the tall, bearded one told me.

So my students and I went to the café adjacent and parked ourselves there. The café was empty too, like some ghost ship in the middle of the Mediterranean.

We chatted and ordered coffee. When it was eleven, the chanting started and I suggested we go in and find seats, just in case it got busy. This possibility was confirmed by the waiter when I told him how empty the whole place seemed. "They all show up at a quarter to midnight, just in time to leave!"

I wondered what he was talking about. The service would last well past midnight.

We strolled inside and lit candles. At first, we settled on chairs in the main sanctuary but we realized we'd have better views by going up the steps to an inner balcony, so we did. A few souls were scattered there; hardly anyone took notice of the foreigners in their midst.

At midnight, the lights suddenly turned off and the priest came out of the altar area with a huge, almost Olympic-sized torch. Suddenly throngs with thick candles crushed around him, anxious to get the flames symbolizing the risen body of Jesus. Then the priest marched to the outside steps of the church. One of my students went to the stained glass windows and gasped at what she saw outside.

I went up to see what the fuss was about and saw a huge throng of people in the outside landing of the church stretching as far as the eye could see. From where in Gawd's name did they abruptly appear?

Their candles lit, it seemed like a scene out of *The DaVinci Code*.

The priest returned and resumed the service inside. I saw the people outside scattering, although a fair number of them remained on the landing, listening to the service that was broadcast via loudspeakers set up around the small plaza.

I watched the people from my perch above, seeing all the movements, including the boredom, the yawns, the forced penitence that added up to a carefully orchestrated scene of annual performance.

The chanting of the "psalti" was powerful yet strangely cold. It was as if everyone was repeating a tired ritual.

The three young priests who performed the mass seemed genuine enough; they had not yet been smitten by cynicism. I imagined they still had some interesting theological discussions when they got together for coffee; the old buggers, the retired priests, probably spoke of God as if He were a demented old dictator put out to pasture.

I did not come to have an epiphany this night and yet somehow one came.

And in the strangest of moments.

My eye caught a young woman in a white dress seemingly out of the 1950s with bright-purple ballerina flats. There were many other souls in the place but somehow my eye stopped on her. Maybe because she seemed so alone, matching my own feelings of being in Greece.

I guessed she was in her mid-twenties, perhaps younger. There was a sense of sadness about her, and when she curled up to sit down from standing on her feet the whole time on the marble steps of the altar, she suddenly seemed ten years old at that moment, perhaps right before crying over some pain in her life.

I tried to imagine what her life would be like in a few years: married, with children, pushing a pram in downtown Ioannina with a husband that sometimes came home early from work but often not. She would be alone in the house, unless she had a job that at least took her away for a few hours a day—teaching perhaps, or even as a secretary to some local big-wig.

And it was then that it hit me: the church was really here for her. Not for me, not for all the other lost middle-aged types;

smart, perhaps worldly, yet often impractical, and too honest with ourselves, so that we live in a state of perpetual war with everything, including our souls, our surroundings, our futures.

No, the church was not built for us losers. It was built for her and all she represents: the happy, beaming, hopeful Greece, the one that charms and prays and finds joy even in difficulty. The one with warmth and forgiveness and blindness to evil. The one that sees life in a context of goodness and not a battleground to be fought over and changed.

No, she is the face of the church and on her kindness is the church built, is the church alive, is the church part of Greece.

It's a strange epiphany to have, since the church is an all-male enclave, yet it suddenly seemed so true to me. All the males in the place, save the priests and the psalti, could disappear and it would not make a lick of difference; the women would remain and it is for them that it would justify its existence.

One-thirty approached and the communion had not started. I was too tired and so were my students. I asked if they wanted to continue, and they said no. So we got up, looked below at the altar one last time and made a beeline escape.

In a few minutes I was back in the guesthouse and watched the *Life of Pi* about the existence of God. Somehow, that seemed appropriate.

What is Greece Now?

Athens, June 7

It's hard to say good-bye to this spit of a place called Greece that was my home for the first eight years of my life, that brought me into this world, that formed me indelibly. Even now as I write this, my heart aches from pain, sadness, and tears. This is hardly the same country that my family left a few decades ago; we were scared, lonely, hopeful, without any preparation for arriving in the United States.

Now I return to Greece in the same way I order pizza for home delivery. The problem, since I always try to make sense of my time here, is to separate the personal from the public.

My family left Greece in a deeply impoverished state, with a military junta that had just suspended democracy and taken power. Now I return to visit Greece despite its recent economic meltdown, when it has become a long-standing member of the European Union and the euro currency. People have automobiles, cell phones and all the toys of modern civilization. It increasingly looks to the east for economic salvation; the plethora of Chinese and Russian tourists in the streets of Athens are overwhelming. Last year at this time, tourists were few; this year, the numbers have swelled. As the country struggles to right itself after four years of a devastating economic depression, the sense that it lacks direction is palpable. No one is sure where it's heading. What role will it play in Europe, in the eastern Aegean, as a bridge to the Middle East?

The tourists come for the sun and beaches and return with trinkets made in China, having eaten too much and taken too many photos—and what have they learned? What have they gained?

Greece once gave the world its art, culture, and science. It transformed civilization. Now it gives away its "village salad" and "mousaka" and fake plaster glass holders, and the world yawns.

No one will recognize this country in a few years; the discovery of natural gas and oil in its waters may turn Greece into another Norway. But it will come with a price. What few see is that as the nation becomes increasingly a plaything of the dominant superpowers (once the United States, now more and more China and Russia), the gut of Greece metastasizes into a public beach for the planet's inhabitants. The few tourists who see beyond the

Potemkin villages may penetrate a veil of spiritual depth and cultural memory, but it's too much work for many.

I am sad for this country, because in our Disneyfied world today we've lost the ability to make sense of a nation and its people by something resembling deeper reflection. We engage the surface of superficiality and call that wisdom.

Greece offers so much more, yet fewer and fewer choose to see it.

And so it stumbles into the future—with many millions of tourists arriving this year, to eat, to see, to suntan, to collapse into exhaustion.

Meanwhile, that which makes Greece a tender reminder that beauty and wonder are contained not just in pretty landscapes, but also in the human heart, fades.

Still, some of us are around to keep that flame alive.

"Fuehrer Arrested"

Seattle, October 1

The arrest of Golden Dawn leader Nikos Michaloliakos last Saturday on charges of running a criminal organization, stunned Greece. The smug-faced Michaloliakos defiantly lifted his handcuffed hands to cameras to show that he was not bothered by the arrest. In the late 1970s, he was jailed for various offenses, including in 1976 for assaulting reporters. He was the first arrested on Saturday; 5:30 A.M. to be precise. Party spokesman, Ilias Kasidiaris, was also arrested. As Kasidiaris arrived at police headquarters, according to *Kathimerini*, he shouted "Nothing will bend us, long live Greece!" Two other GD members of Parliament turned themselves over to police the same day.

The arrests seemed impossible just a few days ago, so Greece has turned a new chapter. What led to this? It was the stabbing death of thirty-four-year-old Greek rapper Pavlos Fyssas, who goes by the stage name of "Killah P.", that woke the country. While it's interesting to note that it took the violent death of a Greek at the hands of a GD supporter, and not the 800 other incidents of abuse (verbal and physical) against immigrants, to finally rouse the Greek state to action, nevertheless it seemed a necessary cause.

At the same time, there have been arrests, investigations and resignations in the country's military and police staff. It's common knowledge that GD received moral and training support from many members of the nation's defense apparatus.

Even many Greek Orthodox clergy support the party.

With Fyssas's death, Greece reached a turning point. To ignore the killing like it did all the other incidents would invite complete chaos.

GD is the most nihilistic and bloodthirsty of all Europe's extreme right-wing parties. Marine Le Pen's right-wing National Front in France works within the parliamentary system. GD would do anything to destroy Greek parliament. From the moment its eighteen deputies arrived in Parliament, they have sought to disrupt it and spoil it as best as they could—bringing guns into the chamber, insulting other deputies, making outrageous accusations—even doing the Hitler salute in the hallowed chamber.

Now its leaders will spend a few days in jail while awaiting the prosecutors. It's time for them to do a little reflection and quiet time in prison. It won't change them, it may make them even more defiant, but at least now they'll have to warm to their resting place that for many will last years and decades.

The damage the party has done to Greece, its image and reputation, will take decades to erase. Their ideas may never die, it's one aspect of the human condition that we keep stupidities and savagery alive, but at least they may be marginalized.

Many suspect that the Greek government of Prime Minister

Antonis Samaras arrived at the decision to arrest them because they realized if they didn't there may have been a military coup. Rumors of such have been floating around conspiracy circles in Greece for some time. This past week they gathered apace. And Samaras faced another death knell of democracy in Greece if he did not act.

Greece is saved, barely, for now.

Grisly deaths of GD members brings empathy

Seattle, November 7

On Friday evening, November 1, 2013, four Golden Dawn members hung around the front entrance to the GD office in a working-class neighborhood in Athens. Two men passed them on a motorcycle but stopped some yards away. They dismounted their motorcycle and walked towards the four GD members. As they did, one of them whipped out a gun and began firing. Within seconds, two GD members were dead on the sidewalk, another seriously injured, and the fourth escaped.

Not more than two weeks before, on September 20, 2013, the government of Prime Minister Antonis Samaras decided to re-move police protection of GD's offices, whereas it normally pro-tects Greek political parties.

The two assailants escaped, and as of this moment have not been caught. The third GD member still lies in critical condition in a hospital, but it seems he will live.

The news shocked Greece; not only for the brazen act, but the worry that there may be a return to earlier decades of ugly ur-ban violence. Terrorist groups like 17 November terrorized the city and the nation, and the thought is now that with political ex-tremism on the rise, thanks mostly to Golden Dawn, a new bloody chapter in the nation's history may soon be written.

More stunning is the empathetic outpouring of support that GD received after the shooting deaths. It was the major story on all main Greek news outlets. Where just a few weeks ago they were condemned by many as a thuggish mafia organization, now suddenly they were martyrs to the cause of free speech.

There is irony here; too much, in fact, to get into this short space. For the past few years, GD terrorized immigrants and liberal groups, attacking, beating and in the case of Pavlos Fyssas the rapper, stabbing to death, with many Greeks remaining unmoved.

With the brutal deaths of their own members, GD cried foul. The two young dead GD members became martyrs to the neo-Nazi cause, rather than victims of an extreme political climate that raises the temperature of instability in Greece and brings with it worrisome concern about where all this madness goes.

For years, Greek political elites watched the emergence of GD and did nothing about it. Hints by the Greek secret service that the party's phones were tapped and movements followed had done nothing to quell the fear that GD was tolerated and perhaps even accepted within the police and military forces of the country.

Now its head lies in prison awaiting trial for running a criminal organization, yet many worry that the charges against the organization will not stand up in a court trial. If acquitted, the Greek government may no longer be in a position to stop the GD neo-Nazi bandwagon from becoming a tsunami. There is a cancer upon the nation and it spreads.

The deaths of the GD members are both a tragedy and a symbol of where Greece stands today. The economics of the country are touted by the Greek government as improving. In reality, manufacturing continues to fall and were it not for the bumper crop of tourists to Greece this year (thanks to turmoil in Egypt and Turkey), the country would be in even worse shape.

As I close this book and look ahead, I see some rays of hope but also darkening clouds. Greece may return to tepid growth next year, and as the global economy slowly improves, this may help further. Yet politically I see pitfalls and dangers everywhere. The Samaras government may be brought down, bringing in new elections and the possibility of wrangling over the memorandum or the agreement between Greece and its international lenders. The Athens stock market, apparently the best performer in the world for the month of October, may react negatively. Europe may finally say enough is enough and pull the plug on Greece's use of the euro. New turmoil sets in and Greece starts from square zero. It's not a hopeful vision, but perhaps a realistic one.

2014

Choosing Greece's Future

Seattle, February 3, 2014

Greece no longer commands front-page headlines in American media. For many observers, this seems good new: the crisis in Greece must be over. The truth is much more convoluted. Rather than indicating Greece is back to normal (however defined), it may be the lull before the storm for this Mediterranean nation.

Hints of an improving economy no longer hemorrhaging trickle in. Consumer confidence is up, retail sales show a recent tepid climb, and the unemployment rate may soon start edging downward. Greece had a bumper tourist crop in 2013, with over 17 million tourists flocking to the country. (Worth cheering, but by way of comparison, that figure equals the yearly tourist visits to Paris alone!)

Beneath the surface, the monster of chaos stirs. For the past four years, since the first bailout agreement between the country's international lenders and Greece took place in 2010, the nation has more or less been governed by outside parties: the International Monetary Fund, the European Commission, and the European Bank. No major decision takes place in Greece without the approval of the troika.

The political toll of this outside control now reaches a crisis stage as the coalition government that has ruled Greece since 2012 teeters on the edge of collapse. Leftist SYRIZA, headed by the young Alexis Tsipras, who turns 40 this summer, is poised to take over running the country from Prime Minister Antonis Samaras's New Democracy. Samaras steadfastly claims no new elections will be called before his governing mandate runs out in 2016, but few believe him. Samaras governs with the liberal

PASOK party, but both his ND and PASOK do not poll well and are shrinking.

Elections for the European Parliament take place this May and if SYRIZA comes out on top, as expected, look for a no-confidence vote in the Greek parliament soon after. Then the country will go to the polls. All normal, right?

Nothing about Greek politics is normal. Splinter parties now flourish with a new one seemingly born every month (as I write this, today a new party is announced, a successor to the "New Day" party created last year). Politicians sense blood and now circle around a weakened Samaras. The Prime Minister stopped taking orders from the troika in autumn 2013, which angered officials of the European Union, thinking he assumed that the troika did not want to see left-wing SYRIZA in power. The troika was not amused by his decision.

Even as euro-pols like Germany's Finance Minister smile and passionately claim their support for Greece, behind the scenes they are furious with the coalition for slowing down the reform. Even if SYRIZA wins an election, the agreements must be adhered to. They reminded Samaras of this but he had nothing to counter them. Greece desperately needs between 10 and 20 billion euros (roughly $14 billion to $28 billion) to continue as a viable nation-state. Without further reform, Greece will lose out on the third bailout from the troika, with complete bankruptcy and almost certain exit from the Eurozone to follow.

Two-faced Greece shows an improving Greek economy on one side while the hidden side masks a cancer not responding to chemotherapy. The patient may be improving, only to soon collapse into coma.

There is the possibility that Samaras may find the courage inside to push through the last of the necessary reforms, in which case Greece will be on track to receive additional financial support from the troika. If so, while he may go down in defeat in snap elections, the road to recovery will be cemented, and when Tsipras takes office, unless he declares open warfare on the Europeans, stability will be ensured.

I like to think the latter will take place, but my heart worries that judging from Greece's history, chaos will rear its ugliness before cooler heads prevail. I hope I am wrong.

Acknowledgements

This book came from the efforts and help of many wonderful, supporting individuals. They deserve great recognition.

Samson X. Lim is the student who helped me put together the blog from which these entries come. He encouraged me to write the blog, and in fact pushed me to do so. And his help and thoughtful comments along the way made it a joy for me to continue, even in those moments when it seemed like a waste of time. He deserves the biggest credit of all for starting what later became this book.

My students in the 2012 study abroad program in Northern Greece provided me with inspiration to think about my surroundings in a way that I perhaps might not have had if I wrote these pieces without anyone around. In a way, their presence reminded me of what was so beautiful and challenging about Greece. It's hard to break down national barriers, more so today than ever before, yet at no time in human history has it been as necessary.

I also thank the folks at the Stavros Niarchos Center at the University of Ioannina for their hospitality and genuine warmth in hosting me and my students during our nearly three month stay in Ioannina. In particular, I am indebted to Gianna Fotou who came to be an invaluable asset and a joy to work with. Thanks also to George Vthokakis for the use of his excellent photographs.

Over the years I've had some unpleasant experiences with editors and publishers. First of all, it's hard to get a book published these days; more and more books are done, so I began to wonder if I really belong in that arena. I still wonder, but if it was not for Phil Haldeman, the publisher of this book, and his constant support, it would never have seen the light of day. His painstaking efforts to prepare the book for publication deserve special recognition.

I am also grateful to my family, including Helen Lagos, Katerina Lagos and Nektaria Klapaki, for their love and support.

And thanks to those who read this book!